GETTING TO THE HEART OF EMPLOYEE ENGAGEMENT

THE POWER AND PURPOSE OF IMAGINATION AND FREE WILL IN THE WORKPLACE

GETTING TO THE HEART OF EMPLOYEE ENGAGEMENT

THE POWER AND PURPOSE OF IMAGINATION AND FREE WILL IN THE WORKPLACE

LES LANDES

iUniverse, Inc.
Bloomington

Getting to the Heart of Employee Engagement
The Power and Purpose of
Imagination and Free Will in the Workplace

iUniverse books may be ordered through booksellers or by contacting:

iUniverse
1663 Liberty Drive
Bloomington, IN 47403
www.iuniverse.com
1-800-Authors (1-800-288-4677)

Because of the dynamic nature of the Internet, any web addresses or links contained in this book may have changed since publication and may no longer be valid. The views expressed in this work are solely those of the author and do not necessarily reflect the views of the publisher, and the publisher hereby disclaims any responsibility for them.

Any people depicted in stock imagery provided by Thinkstock are models, and such images are being used for illustrative purposes only.

Certain stock imagery © Thinkstock.

ISBN: 978-1-4759-4799-1 (sc)
ISBN: 978-1-4759-4801-1 (e)
ISBN: 978-1-4759-4800-4 (dj)

Library of Congress Control Number: 2012916493

Printed in the United States of America

iUniverse rev. date: 12/26/2012

This book is dedicated
to
David K. Berlo,

a brilliant teacher
who shared his profound wisdom
with
elegant simplicity.

Contents

Preface

How many times have you scratched your head or pulled your hair out wondering why it's so hard to get people in the workplace to pull consistently in the same direction—let alone doing it with a compelling, common sense of purpose, passion, and commitment to excellence? I've spent most of my professional life working on that challenge, developing an array of solutions that are grounded mainly in the fields of communication, organizational psychology, and systems thinking.

For the most part, those solutions have been quite effective in the work I've done both as the head of corporate communications for a large international food company and as a consultant working with client organizations of all types and sizes. Despite those successes, though, I've always felt a longing to get at the heart—the essential elemental truths—of what gets people tuned in, turned on, and eager to go the extra mile for the mutual benefit of themselves and the organizations they work for. I'm convinced that understanding those truths will help people get past the stumbling blocks that so often derail and discourage efforts to tap into the full-blown potential of employee engagement.

At the risk of sounding a bit lofty, I've compared my quest to Einstein's pursuit of the elusive unified field theory, the Holy Grail of physics. He searched for it most of his life to explain the connection between all of the forces of the universe in a single equation. He never found that theory, but his famed equation $E=mc2$ was a huge leap in that direction.

When I started writing this book, I wasn't sure what my single "equation" might turn out to be for employee engagement, so I focused initially on laying out the core parts of the big picture. It seemed to me that it might be rooted in the uniquely human qualities of imagination and free will, but by themselves, those qualities certainly were not new, and they weren't sufficient to shed significant new light on the subject.

Then it hit me. The answer is rooted in the *intrinsic relationship* between imagination and free will. The secret to employee engagement lies not merely in our capacity to imagine and choose, but in understanding how those qualities are inseparably interrelated.

That was a breakthrough moment for me, and it sparked a flood of insight about why organizations struggle with employee engagement. It also opened the door to understanding how nurturing the combined power of imagination and free will in the workplace can allow employees to contribute the greatest and be the best that human beings are designed to be.

For those of you who share my passion for the power and potential of employee engagement that transcends the norm, I hope the ideas in this book will challenge and inspire you to explore new ways to create the kind of organization where employees love to work and customers love doing business.

Acknowledgments

Albert Einstein was more than a great scientist. He was also a wry sage with a great sense of humor and a flare for irony. "The secret to creativity is knowing how to hide your sources," he once said.

I want to acknowledge that many of the creative concepts in this book have been colored by similar ideas that preceded them, and I want to recognize the people who have influenced the thinking that led to this book's creation. Having said that, I must also point out that the more people you meet, the more you read, the more you learn, and the older you get, the more likely you are to forget someone along the way. If I have failed to cite someone's contributions in this list of acknowledgments, please accept my apologies for the oversight.

First and foremost, I need to acknowledge the late, great Dr. David K. Berlo, the man to whom this book is dedicated and the person who has influenced my thinking more than anyone I have ever known. His brilliance was unparalleled, and his command of the English language was breathtaking. When I describe his intellect to people, I do so playfully by saying that, on a scale of 1 to 10—with 10 being the highest—David was a 25.

He was a university president, a business consultant, a communication theorist, a philosopher, a psychologist, and much more—including a dear friend. Despite the many prestigious positions he held and accolades he received during his lifetime, he always preferred to call himself simply a teacher. In fact, up to the last year of his life, he claimed that he always entered the word *teacher* in the box on his tax return labeled

"Occupation." I have never known a better one, and I am forever indebted to him for what he taught me over the years.

I also want to acknowledge Ken Blanchard. His landmark book *The One-Minute Manager* (and others that followed in his path) blazed the trail for numerous authors like me who were inspired by Blanchard's success in writing real stories about real people with very human, heartfelt, and important things to say about employee engagement. Coincidentally, David Berlo was a friend of Ken's as well and also influenced some of his writings over the years.

Much of the thinking in the book comes from the work of organizational gurus like W. Edwards Deming, Joseph Juran, Phil Crosby, Douglas McGregor, and Jackson Grayson. Jack founded the American Productivity and Quality Center and was a principal architect of the Baldrige National Quality Award. I had the privilege of working with Jack during the early years of the quality movement in this country, and some of his thinking has influenced me as well.

Closer to home, another big influence has been Wainwright Industries, based in St. Peters, Missouri. Their journey from being a traditional manufacturer of automotive and aerospace components to winning the 1994 Baldrige National Quality Award provided a real-world showcase of how to translate transformational organizational theory into hard-nosed, practical systems and processes. After winning the Baldrige Award, president Don Wainwright opened the doors of the company to the world and traveled extensively across the globe so others—including Wainwright's competitors—could learn and benefit from what the company had implemented so successfully. Don and I worked together on several projects to highlight the work of the company, and he graciously spent many hours with me sharing the Wainwright success story.

Another pivotal figure from Wainwright Industries is Mike Simms, who was educated as a meteorologist, became a plant manager, then turned to business consulting—though he really should have been a Sunday preacher. His special combination of passion, insight, and practical experience has contributed substantially to how this book has taken shape. We continue to work together in bringing the principles and processes described in this book to clients across the country.

I must also acknowledge Roger Fritz, a former colleague and friend who passed away in 2006 after a three-year battle with brain cancer. Next to David Berlo, Roger may have had the most expansive mind and penetrating insight of anyone I've ever known. His own book, *Living an Aspiring Life*, coauthored by Irene Underwood and published just before his death, is a touching tribute to people transcending the circumstances of their lives.

I would also like to acknowledge numerous other people who have contributed to this book in many ways, large and small. They include Tom Heuerman, Dick Palmer, Suzsanne Singer, Cynthia Bishop, Sharon Mackay, Jim Lukaszewski, Deanna Pelfrey, Jed Ramura, Marie Casey, Bill Seyle, Frans VanOudenallen, Jay Fedora, Steve Finkelstein, Steve Lawler, Pete Snyder, Doug Silsbee, Michelle Golden, Jack Pyle, Barbara Carnes, Eva Dahm, Tami Craig-Schilling, Glynn Young, Ann Tretter, Diane Gayeski, Roger Vorhies, Gus Schaus, Blair Forlaw, Jim Shaffer, Dixie Gillaspie, Gill Wagner, Jim Holtje, Cara Koen, Kristi Mackansi, Eileen Floyd, Laura Lawson, Kathe Sweeny, Johanna Vondeling, Kathy Cramer and the rest of the gang at the Cramer Institute, Maril MacDonald and her team at Gagen-MacDonald, Cindy Solomon, Patrick Carpenter, Lynn Manternach, Dawn Bashara, Susie Benigas and David Grossman. In one way or another, they have all made important contributions to the character and substance of the book.

Last, but far from least, I want to acknowledge my wife, Dawn, whose patience, encouragement, and superb editing skills have been so vital to this book and much of my other writing over the years.

L. L.

Introduction

On June 24, 1980, NBC aired a documentary program that would eventually change the course of American business: *If Japan Can, Why Can't We?* Somehow, over the span of a few short years, the tiny Asian country had managed to rise from a poor-quality producer of low-end trinkets to a major manufacturer of high-quality automobiles and electronics sold worldwide.

When NBC correspondent Lloyd Dobbins set out to find the people responsible for that transformation, he kept hearing about a man who had become a legend in Japan but who was virtually unknown in the United States. To Dobbins's surprise, this miracle worker was an American. What's more, the man was eighty years old, deemed over the hill and out of touch by the few people in this country who knew him. His name was Dr. W. Edwards Deming, and on the night of the broadcast, America finally started to pay attention.

Deming's message—one that eventually made its way throughout most of corporate America in some form or another—was twofold. First, excellence requires a disciplined approach based on rigorous management systems and measurement methods such as statistical process control. His second message was about people. He asserted that employees could contribute far more to improving an organization's performance than most companies appreciated or enabled, and his success in Japan proved it.

Ever since that eventful broadcast more than three decades ago, the business market has been flooded with books and articles attempting to shed greater light on how to optimize the potential of people in creating high-performance organizations. While many of the ideas offered about how to crack the code of employee engagement have been very good, the research that has been conducted on the results and impact has not been encouraging.

Multiple studies have shown that most major improvement initiatives aimed at transforming organizational cultures have failed to produce any meaningful results. In many cases, companies acknowledge that their improvement efforts have backfired and made things worse. Most of the publicity about notable transformations has come from a relatively small number of anecdotal successes.

While those limited examples provide clear evidence of what can be accomplished by boosting employee engagement, many workers in US companies remain largely disenchanted and disengaged—and their potential remains largely untapped. The numbers reported in the *Gallup Management Journal*'s Employee Engagement Index, recorded in October 2011, are quite discouraging:

- 29 percent of employees are *actively engaged* in their jobs
- 52 percent are *not engaged*
- 19 percent are *actively disengaged*

What's more, Gallup estimates that the "actively disengaged" segment of the workforce costs US businesses $300 billion per year. In part, those dismal results stem from a failure to get at the root of human nature and how it affects motivation and performance in the workplace. The concepts presented in *Getting to the Heart of Employee Engagement* provide a new foundation for understanding what it takes to get employees more fully engaged in the workplace. The book is based on a provocative premise that goes to the core of what makes human beings unique: the *intrinsic relationship* between our capacity for *imagination* and our *free will* to make choices that are not dictated by the imprinted code that controls the behavior of all other living creatures.

The book is written as a story, a tale of two characters who have a not-so-chance encounter in the halls of a large corporation. One is Tom Payton, a human resources and employee communications manager, who is searching for answers—and seeking a promotion. The other is

David Kay, an enigmatic consultant who mysteriously guides Tom on a journey of discovery.

Over the course of several days, Tom and David's conversations run the gamut from the silly to the sublime, from the humorous to the serious, and from the novelty of Barney, the purple dinosaur, to the elegant wisdom of Henry David Thoreau. Together, the two men explore essential topics relevant to employee engagement, such as continuous improvement, performance development, communication, and more.

Each time they meet, David illuminates, and Tom is enlightened—although not without occasional tension and struggle along the way. Their relationship ultimately transforms with a dramatic surprise ending that reveals to Tom more about himself and the nature of people in the workplace than he could have ever imagined on that fateful day when he and David first met.

The ideas captured in their dialogue provide approaches to employee engagement that are based on insights from historically significant thinkers in various organizational disciplines. They also draw on proven practices used by top-performing companies, including winners of the Baldrige National Quality Award.

The book unfolds as follows:

- The Prologue sets the stage for the story.
- Chapter 1 introduces elemental truths about the difference between human beings and other living creatures, including the essential connection between imagination and free will.
- Chapter 2 explores and challenges mistaken notions many people have about employee attitudes regarding control in the workplace.
- Chapter 3 introduces a counterintuitive approach to optimizing employee involvement in continuous improvement and generating the greatest impact.
- Chapter 4 lays out basic truths and realities about human nature and the workplace that go against the grain of common wisdom.
- Chapter 5 provides a step-by-step process for working with employees to enable them to contribute to their fullest.

- Chapter 6 explains the importance of getting rid of the traditional appraisal process in order to foster a genuine culture of growth and development.
- Chapter 7 looks at the crucial element of trust in the workplace—what it is, how to get it, and why it's so important.
- Chapter 8 outlines the criteria and characteristics of an effective organizational communication system, which is essential for employee engagement.
- Chapter 9 reveals our innate understanding for what works and what doesn't when it comes to employee engagement.
- Chapter 10 reveals the outcome of Tom's quest to serve in a capacity that allows him to lead the company in transforming its employee engagement efforts.
- Appendix A provides a summary of the core concepts at the heart of the book.
- Appendix B presents a detailed description of a proven world-class system used by a number of Baldrige National Quality Award winners for engaging employees in systematic continuous improvement.
- Appendix C offers the design for a measurement communication system that builds on the traditional foundation of dashboards and scorecards.

Several factors drove my choice to present the ideas in the book as a story. First and foremost, most people like reading stories more than basic business text. Stories also help to heighten the human reality of what's at stake in providing employees with a workplace environment that allows them to do and be their very best. Achieving effective employee engagement is not a straight-line process. It's messy. It's emotional. And it's frustrating. Showing the drama of how people work through those challenges illuminates the path to a high-performance culture as much as the solutions themselves.

Enjoy!

Prologue

T om Payton is a middle-aged assistant vice president who has been working in the human resources and employee communication department of a major corporation for ten years. During the past few months, he has been trying to develop new policies, practices, and processes to boost employee engagement and improve working relationships among employees and between departments.

Despite his best efforts, every step Tom has taken up to now has left him uninspired. Some of the ideas look promising, but nothing seems like a real breakthrough. He is concerned that if he doesn't come up with some bold thinking and fresh ideas soon, the plan that senior management has asked him to develop will wind up as a nice try that produces only marginal results.

Just as Tom is about to pack up his briefcase and head home for the day, his phone rings. His boss, Marie Prescott, the vice president of human resources and employee communication, is calling to ask if she can talk with him in her office before he takes off.

Tom and Marie have been close colleagues since he started with the company, and they have great respect for one another. She is a big player in HR, recognized nationally as a leader in the profession. She also carries considerable weight with senior management, and when she speaks, they all listen closely and follow her lead.

Tom has a sense that something hasn't been quite right with Marie lately, though. He hasn't seen as much of her laser-like focus as usual. As he approaches her office, he decides this is as good a time as any to find out what is going on with her. It doesn't take him long to find out.

After a few pleasantries, Marie tells Tom that she will be leaving the company soon to take a post working for the governor as the state's new head of workforce development.

While Tom is excited for Marie, he can't help wondering what her departure will mean for him and his career. Before he has a chance to raise the subject, Marie tells Tom that she has urged senior management to appoint him to her job. But there's a catch. While the senior management team thinks highly of Tom, they are not sure he's ready for the top spot in the department, so they want to look at some other candidates as well.

Tom knows their expectations are high, and he will have to put on a strong performance during the interview process if he is going to have a real shot at the VP position. Despite Marie's endorsement, Tom feels unsure about his chances. All of the thinking and searching he has done during the past few months have left him feeling frustrated and disillusioned. Still, he is certain that the answers he needs are out there somewhere—perhaps even closer than he realizes. To see them, he just needs a fresh perspective.

As Tom leaves Marie's office to head home, a bizarre notion occurs to him. People put cheese in a trap when they want to catch a rat. But what if he turned things around? What if the rat set a trap to catch the cheese? It was a silly notion, of course, but as he turned the idea over in his mind on the drive home, the playfulness of the image seemed to shift his feelings and thoughts about his dilemma.

As Tom walks into the house, he hears his wife, Jennifer, a marketing consultant, on the phone. It sounds like she is dealing with a late-night client crisis. He walks over and gives her a peck on the cheek. As she smiles and continues her conversation, he thinks about how much they have invested in their careers. At times, they have wondered if it has been worth the effort. Every time they talk about it, though, they realize how much passion they both have for their work. And despite the challenges and demands it has placed on their time, they have managed to create the kind of life they always wanted for themselves and their three children.

When she hangs up the phone, Tom gets right to the point. Jennifer listens intently as Tom relays the story of what happened with Marie and their discussion about the challenges with the employee engagement plan. Sharing Marie's confidence in Tom's talents, Jennifer tells him she would bet on him any day to come up with a plan that will make a big impression on senior management.

Later that night, as Tom lies in bed, his head swirls with a flood of ideas about what lies ahead for him and his engagement plan. His thoughts shoot one way and then another. The last thing he remembers thinking about before falling asleep is the need to get in touch with some elemental truths—to look beyond the obvious and beneath the surface. Somehow, he's sure that is where he will find what he's looking for.

The story that unfolds in the following pages describes Tom's journey of discovery as he seeks to unveil the secrets to extraordinary employee engagement.

chapter 1
What Makes People Work

"Okay. Elemental truths," Tom muttered to himself as he walked down the hall to his office the next morning. "Is that what I've been missing? Is that really why it's been so tough to get people fully on board? What does that mean, anyway?"

"If you take a breath for a second, I might be able to help with those questions," came a reply from out of the blue.

Tom jumped in surprise. He looked up and saw someone standing at the door of a nearby office. The man seemed vaguely familiar, but Tom couldn't place him. He was embarrassed to discover he had been talking loudly enough for someone to hear him.

"Sorry," Tom said, "I didn't know anybody else was around. My name's Tom Payton."

"I know," the man said, reaching out to shake Tom's hand.

"Have we met before?" Tom asked.

"I'm David Kay. I'm a consultant here on a short-term assignment. I'll just be here for a few days." David continued before Tom could ask him what he was working on. "And by the way ... no apologies necessary. Sometimes, a thought is just too big to keep locked up inside your head."

"Isn't that the truth!" said Tom.

"Mind if I ask what you're puzzled about?" asked David.

"Oh, it's just people stuff," replied Tom.

"From my experience, that's the biggest stuff of all in most companies," said David. "It can get pretty complicated."

"You can say that again," said Tom. Maybe it was the mood of the moment or maybe it was something about David, but Tom suddenly found himself eager to open up and talk about the employee engagement challenges he was facing.

"Right now, I'm feeling pretty overwhelmed, to be honest with you," he continued. "I'm in the human resources and employee communication department, and we've got some big changes in front of us. We just started working on an organization-wide performance improvement effort. It looks promising, but the head of HR and communication who's been leading the project—she's my boss—just told me she's leaving. It's going to be a big shock for everyone."

"So, what are you planning to do now?" asked David as he turned and started down the hall. Tom fell in easily beside him.

"I'm not sure," Tom replied. "I've been here for about ten years, and when the CEO gave us the green light to put together a new employee engagement plan, I thought I'd died and gone to heaven. Now with Marie quitting, I feel like I'm headed the other direction—if you know what I mean."

"So when Marie leaves, where does that leave you and the plan?" asked David.

"I don't know," said Tom. "Marie is a heavy hitter in HR and communication circles, and she carries a lot of weight with senior management. She did a great job of convincing them that we had to do some pretty dramatic things if we were going to stay competitive in the industry."

"Do you think they're going to change their minds now that Marie's leaving?" David asked.

"I doubt it," said Tom. "But they're going to be looking for someone very strong to fill her shoes, and you know what it's like—someone new comes in, and he feels like he has to make his own mark. He brings in his own ideas, and everything we've been working on gets shoved aside. It's the old NIH syndrome. Know what I mean?"

"Not invented here," David said with a smile, nodding thoughtfully.

"I guess you can't blame a person for doing that. I'd probably do the same thing if I was brought in to lead a big change effort."

"Any chance of that happening?" asked David.

"What's that?" Tom asked in return.

"You taking over and leading the change effort," David replied.

"Well, I am throwing my hat in the ring," said Tom hesitantly. "Marie likes my work, and she's encouraged me to go for it. She even put in a good word to management for me."

"That sounds pretty encouraging," said David. "But you don't sound like a guy who's just been given a great opportunity and a strong endorsement to boot."

"Yeah, I know," said Tom. "That's actually what I was muttering about a few minutes ago. I've been in HR and employee communication for quite a while—most of it right here with this company. Marie hired me, and we've done some good work together. But …"

Tom hesitated, appearing to struggle for the right words.

"But," he continued, "I just haven't felt like we were getting to the core of what it's going to take to produce some major breakthroughs in employee performance and development."

"Well, what made you think you needed to make any changes in the first place?" asked David.

"Mainly, it's because our productivity and profitability are lagging behind the industry trends," Tom answered.

"You hear that from a lot of companies these days," said David. He spoke casually but with a let's-cut-to-the-chase look. "I'm sure there was more behind it than that."

Tom was surprised at David's comment. It had hit a nerve, but he still wanted to continue the conversation. Suddenly, David stopped in front of an office that was virtually empty except for a desk, a chair, and a phone.

"Is this where you're going to be hanging out?" Tom asked.

"It's not fancy, but it's home for now," David replied with a smile.

"Mind if I come in for a few minutes?" Tom asked. "If you've got some time, I'd like to tell you more about the plan we're working on and get your reaction to it."

"Grab a seat," David offered. He sat down and waited quietly for Tom to continue.

"So, back to your question … I guess one of my personal reasons for the new engagement plan is because every year I pore over those lists,—you know, like the 100 Best Companies to Work For—and I wonder what they're doing that we're not," Tom said. "Makes you feel a bit jealous, especially when you're in HR."

"I know what you mean," David acknowledged.

"What's more," Tom continued, "most of those companies must've managed to crack the code on how to bring out the best in employee performance because they are also the toughest competitors in the marketplace. That's a potent combination, and it would be great to be part of a company like that. I'm hoping we're on the right path to duplicate that performance, but I'm not sure. Fact is, we've tried some things in the past that haven't worked very well."

"Any idea why?" asked David.

"Why we tried them? Or why they didn't work?"

David laughed. "Both, actually."

"Well, we look around at those high-performance companies—we see how they're operating, how they're working with people. Then we say we need to step up and do what those guys are doing," Tom said. He paused, reflecting for a moment before he continued.

"Actually, I'm not sure I can put my finger on any single reason why we haven't gotten the same results here," said Tom thoughtfully. "But it's pretty easy to see the symptoms. We start doubting that their results are due to people factors, or we don't understand how to do it, or it looks like too much work, or who knows what. So we keep stumbling along, doing basically the same things, just trying to work harder and faster to catch up. Then instead of getting better performance, people get upset—they feel pushed and pressured, and things start to fall apart. That's when management comes out and pronounces that everyone has to rally around the company flag and give 110 percent if they want the company to survive and keep their jobs. It's become a pretty predictable pattern."

"You know, Tom, you're not the only company struggling with that dilemma," said David. "It's fairly common, and almost every one of those organizations has people like you, scratching their heads and asking themselves why people won't get on board."

"Got some ideas about why that might be?" asked Tom.

"Oh, I might have a thought or two," David replied.

"I'm all ears," said Tom eagerly.

"Do you mind if I start by asking you a question?" asked David.

"Fire away," Tom replied.

"What do you think makes human beings distinct from other living creatures on the planet?" asked David. "What sets us apart?"

Tom wasn't sure where David was going with his question, but he was intrigued. "Lots of things," Tom responded quickly. "One of them has to be our intelligence. We're smarter than other animals."

"What makes you so sure about that?" asked David.

"What do you mean?" Tom shot back. "When was the last time you saw a chimp read a novel or balance a checkbook?"

"I'd be careful about that checkbook comparison," David replied, smiling. "I haven't managed to get mine squared away for quite a few years." Both men laughed as David continued.

"Seriously, though, you can look at intelligence a lot of different ways," David said. "Think about it. No one but Spider-Man has been able to figure out how to make anything so fine *and* strong as a spider's web. Have you ever watched a dog work a herd of livestock? Sure looks pretty intelligent to me."

"Okay, then, how about this one?" asked Tom. "Surely you don't believe that animals have souls—that good ones go to heaven and bad ones go to … well, you know."

"I'm not going to speculate about where animals go when they die," said David. "But do animals have souls? I dare you to get into a debate about that with die-hard animal lovers."

"Okay, I give up," said Tom with a smile of resignation. "You're obviously trying to make a point. So what is it? What do you think makes humans different from other animals?"

"Do you have any kids, Tom?" asked David.

"Three of them," Tom replied. "Five, eight, and thirteen."

"That's great," said David. "Are any of them into Barney the purple dinosaur? I know he's not as big with kids these days, but he used to be wildly popular."

Tom rolled his eyes. "You have no idea," he said. "I have to admit I'm not a big fan, but our five-year-old, DJ, is absolutely mesmerized by him. The other two were just as bad when they were his age."

"What do you think Barney's big appeal is with kids? What does he talk about all the time that's so captivating to them?" asked David.

"I can't imagine," said Tom.

"Yes, you can," said David. "In fact, that's the answer."

"What's the answer?" asked Tom.

"The answer to both questions—what's different about human beings, and why kids love Barney," said David.

"You're losing me, David," said Tom with a puzzled look.

David smiled and said softly, almost with a tone of reverence, "It's … imagination. Human beings are uniquely endowed with the capacity to create or process imaginary experiences. We have the gift to imagine things that never were and create things that have never been. All other animals basically take the world the way it comes. They can demonstrate tremendous intelligence—even use rudimentary tools. And they have most of the same basic needs that people do—for food, shelter, love, and affection. But all you have to do is look at something as simple as a pencil, and you realize that the source of almost everything distinctive that human beings have ever achieved is imagination."

"Okay, so humans are like Barney—they have imagination," said Tom with a touch of sarcasm. "Now, what does a purple dinosaur's imagination have to do with employee engagement in a corporation that employs twenty thousand people?"

"More than you think—but not more than you might imagine," said David. "Let me ask you another question: How important is innovation to this company's business strategy in the next few years?"

"It's critical," replied Tom. "And I get your point. Without imagination, it's hard to have innovation, right?"

"Yeah, that's pretty obvious, isn't it?" said David. "But that's only half the story. Imagination only provides the spark for innovation. It takes more than that to get a real fire started. Any idea what that is?"

"Well, you need people to take action on the ideas that their imaginations generate," said Tom.

"That's right," said David. "Otherwise you've got a bunch of ideas with no place to go. Now what does it take for people to get into action?"

"Lots of things," replied Tom. "They need direction and resources; support and encouragement are important, too."

"You're heading down the right path," said David. "But there's something else that comes into play first—something else about people that sets them apart from other animals."

"I'm not sure," said Tom. "Does it have something to do with motivation?"

"You're close," said David. "Do something for me. Finish this phrase: free as a …"

"Bird," Tom replied quickly.

"It never fails. I always get the same answer from people," said David. "Now let me ask you this. What is a bird free to do?"

"Just about anything it wants to do, I guess," replied Tom.

"Are you sure?" David asked with a smile.

"Well, I was until you asked the question," Tom replied, chuckling.

"The truth is, a bird is only free to do one thing, and that's to do what birds are designed to do," said David. "It may look like they're flying around free to do whatever they want, but they're actually programmed to do what they *have* to do—hunt for food, build nests, and make baby birds. That's basically it."

"I think they're also programmed to leave their droppings all over my car," said Tom with a smile.

"Trust me," said David. "They're not picking on you. They unload on all of us once in a while. But it's nothing personal. They're just responding to nature's call, and that's an important difference between people and other animals. People can make choices—choices that may or may not be in tune with the natural order of things. And they're able to do that because of one thing—*free will.*"

"I think I know where you're heading," said Tom. "If people don't feel free to act on their imaginations, you won't get innovation, right?"

"Sounds simple," said David. "But here's something very important about imagination and free will that a lot of people don't think about: one without the other is useless."

"How's that?"

"Think about it, Tom," replied David. "Free will without imagination has no *purpose.* Imagination without free will has no *power.*"

Tom was speechless as he reflected on what David had just said. Was that the elemental truth that he had been searching for?

"That's a powerful idea," Tom said finally after a moment of silence. "I'm struck by how something so simple can be so profound. It makes you realize just how vital it is to give people the space they need to be … well … people."

"It actually goes deeper than that," said David. "If you don't give people room to maneuver, if you don't give them the freedom to take initiative, you'll not only restrict their free will, you'll eventually snuff out their imagination, too. They'll hang up their brains on the coat rack when they walk into work—and they'll pick them up again when they leave at the end of the day. It's just too frustrating for people to have their imaginations churning all day if they have no place to go with the ideas they generate. So they just put their imaginations in park, and once they do, it can be mighty difficult to get them moving again. And, of course, it's their choice to do that if they want."

Tom knew exactly what David was talking about. The company had tried several times during the past couple of years to get employees more engaged in making improvements in the organization. They could see how much impact it was having in other companies. But despite their efforts, he knew that most managers in the company were only giving token acknowledgment to the value of employee ideas for improvement. He hoped David was about to tell him how to get over the hump.

"You've got my attention," said Tom. "Please tell me you're going to give me some ideas on how to break the logjam and keep people's brains engaged."

"Actually, I've got some work to do right now," said David, looking at his watch. "But if you want to come back tomorrow, I'll give you a few examples of how these ideas play out with people in the workplace."

"Sounds great," said Tom. "But can you at least give me a clue about what you mean? You've got me feeling pretty hungry."

"All right, you asked for it," said David. "I'm going to give you an assignment. When you get home tonight, I want you to watch one of your kid's Barney videos."

Tom laughed and grimaced as David continued. "You already know what to look for, right?"

"I can only imagine," replied Tom with a knowing wink. "Okay, I'll do it," he added with a feigned tone of resignation. "And by the way, thanks, David. I've really enjoyed talking with you. This is the first time in a long time that I've felt like I'm cutting through the clutter and getting a clearer idea about what may work here."

"Listen, Tom, this stuff is already in here." David tapped his temple. "It's just a matter of working through it until it all comes together. In the meantime, I'll be around for a while if you need me."

"I don't know what to say other than thank you," Tom replied earnestly, mildly curious about why David was making himself so available. "I hope I'm not taking you away from your assignment."

"My time is your time."

"I really appreciate it, David," Tom said. "This is very important to me—not just because I'd love a shot at Marie's job, but because it is important to the company. I know we really need to get the people puzzle right, and I know it's not easy. So, I'm going to go home tonight and plop down on the floor beside DJ and watch Barney."

"I bet it'll be more fun than you think," David said.

"Maybe so," Tom replied. "But I can guarantee one thing. My kids are going to laugh themselves silly when I tell them what I want to watch. Now that I think about it, I haven't spent much fun time with them lately. Too much on my mind, I guess. Can you imagine how they're going to react?" asked Tom.

"Sure, I can," said David. "It's just human nature."

Imagination without free will has no power. Free will without imagination has no purpose.

chapter 2
Control Is Just Another
Word for Predictability

As Tom walked down the hall past David's office, he caught himself humming the familiar strains of the *Barney and Friends* theme song. Just a few days ago, he had been telling his wife how much the tune grated on his nerves.

"I knew watching Barney would get to you, but you've surpassed my expectations," came a voice from behind him.

Tom turned around to see David walking toward him with a smug grin and a twinkle in his eye.

"What did you expect?" asked Tom. "It was hard enough fighting the purple dinosaur craze before you came along. I decided if you can't beat 'em, you might as well join 'em."

"Were your kids surprised when you sat down to watch Barney?" asked David.

"Uh, *stunned* would be a better word," said Tom, laughing. "Actually, DJ, my five-year-old, was thrilled—he insisted that I sing along to all the songs. Then we had to pretend we were flying on a spaceship past Jupiter and Mars. The older two walked in and just stood there laughing. My wife, on the other hand, threatened to call the doctor."

"Nothing like an understanding spouse, eh?" David teased.

"She's actually pretty remarkable," Tom replied. "She has a way of keeping me grounded in the things that really matter."

"Sounds like you're a pretty lucky guy," David said approvingly. "Do you have a few minutes to sit and talk a bit more?"

"You bet," Tom agreed.

"So, tell me, now that you're a Barney aficionado, what did you think about him?"

"Well, I'd be lying if I said I was transformed by the experience," said Tom. "And I can't say I'm chomping at the bit to get home and see another Barney show. But it did make me wonder why something that seems so silly to me—and to most other adults—is so fixating for kids. I mean, what makes us so different in the way we see the world?"

"Did you try to answer that question?" asked David.

"Yeah, but I didn't come up with anything very profound," Tom replied. "Part of it, I guess, is just that you get more realistic about things as you get older. I mean, if I tried to jump out a window and fly around the neighborhood like Barney did in the video, I'd be dead, right?"

"But let me ask you this," said David. "Do you ever worry that one of your children might decide to jump out a window and try to fly around the neighborhood like Barney does?"

"No, of course not," answered Tom, pausing to reflect on what David had asked. "So what you're saying is that kids don't actually lose touch with reality when they're watching things like Barney or playing with their imaginary friends."

"That's not it at all," said David. "You're missing the point. It has nothing to do with what's real. Don't confuse imagination with *unreality*. Believe me, the things you imagine are just as real as the shoes on your feet. The difference is that the stuff you imagine isn't *natural*. It's not part of the world of nature that is made of stone and wood and flesh and bones—and gravity."

Tom stared out the window with a longing gaze. "I remember running around the neighborhood as a kid playing cops and robbers and pretending I was a great baseball player or a superhero. Sometimes, I'd get so caught up in those other worlds—they seemed very real. But I always knew I had to be home by dinnertime or I was in big trouble. That's the point you're making, right?"

"Sort of," David acknowledged hesitantly. "The point is that kids won't jump out the window because they understand the laws of nature—just like you knew you couldn't stop a speeding bullet," said

David. "And they know there are consequences if you try to break those laws. But what's great about kids—and you really have to get this, Tom—is that they never lose touch with their imagination despite the constraints of the natural world that they have to deal with just like you and me. Thank goodness, some people manage to keep their imaginations thriving even when they become adults, or we'd have to experience life without Mickey Mouse or Cinderella or—"

"Or Barney," added Tom with a smile.

"That's right … or Barney," replied David. "But the implications of imagination go much further than cartoon characters and fairy tales. Remember what I said about a pencil? Even something as simple as that gives you a glimpse into the significance of our ability to imagine. And not only in terms of creative things like art or music or dance. Just think of the power and potential of human imaginings when you see creations like cars and computers and skyscrapers and … well … everything that doesn't occur naturally in the world around us."

Tom thought for a moment about what David had said and then slowly shook his head.

"Boy, you just hit me between the eyes," said Tom. "We keep talking around here about how important it is to be more innovative if we're going to be more competitive. And like you said, imagination is the source of every truly creative, innovative thought we have. It just makes it even more apparent that we're not doing nearly enough to foster it here."

"It's a common problem in most organizations," said David. "And there's a very good reason for it."

"What do you mean?" Tom asked. "Are you saying we *shouldn't* foster imagination?"

"Not at all," David replied. "But I am saying that you'd better not try to turn people loose in the workplace with their imaginations unless you've got a system in place to make sure they don't fly out of control."

"But how do you unleash people's imagination without releasing control?" asked Tom. "Seems like they're contradictory forces."

"Let me ask you this," began David. "Do you think people prefer to operate without any direction and control in their lives?"

Tom was struck by how natural the back-and-forth exchange between him and David seemed. He was also excited that he felt he was working his way toward some vital answers in his search for an effective employee engagement plan.

"Not really," replied Tom. "In fact, it's just the opposite, from what I can tell. When people feel like things are out of control, it actually makes them a bit crazy."

"Sometimes *very* crazy," said David. "Another way to put it is that people want their lives to be predictable. Not always and not in every situation—life would be pretty boring that way. But certainly they want predictability when critical issues are on the line. Very few people are willing to bet the farm on wild ideas."

"Absolutely," said Tom. "That's why I'm amazed when I see how upset people get about some of the controls we put in place around here. All we're trying to do is increase predictability, like you said."

"But think about that, Tom," David countered. "You're missing an important distinction. It's true that people want control and predictability, but they *don't* want to *be* controlled without having any say in the matter. They want a sense of freedom, yes, but not necessarily freedom without limits or responsibilities. They want the freedom to succeed *and* the freedom to make mistakes. In any case, no one wants to feel like a slave to their work or their boss."

"Doesn't that depend on your point of view?" asked Tom. "I mean, one person's slavery can be another person's respect for authority, can't it?"

"You really think so?" David asked. "Imagine you've got a company with talented workers who want to help the company succeed—because their personal fortunes are tied to company success, if for no other reason. Imagine also that you've got a management system in place that dictates all the company policies and controls from the top. The workers are smart people the company selected to be part of the team. Even if these workers enjoy their jobs, do you think they'll respond well to being controlled?"

"I get your point," Tom acknowledged.

"Pretty obvious, eh?" David said. "What's more, if you have supervisors acting like parents or prison guards to enforce those controls, it only makes matters worse. Usually, you don't get outright rebellion—

it's more subtle than that. But it can still be very damaging. People just put their performance on cruise control at whatever level you dictate —and that's all you'll ever get. Not an ounce of effort more. That's especially true if they see a potential downside in it for them."

"Yeah, I can relate to that," said Tom. "I'll never forget when we launched a big initiative to increase efficiency a few years ago. Reengineering was the craze at the time, so we decided that's how we'd couch the whole thing. It wasn't long before it became a dirty word because employees saw it as just a euphemism for reducing headcount."

"I'll bet that's how the management team thought about it for the most part, too," said David.

"That's probably true," said Tom. "We never really got around to devoting as much thinking and energy to the other aspects of reengineering."

"Few organizations ever do," said David.

"So how do you strike the right balance between freedom and control in an organization as large as ours?" asked Tom. "You can't have everyone involved in all of the decision making all of the time."

"No one wants to be involved in *all* the decision making," said David, "not even the head of your company—in fact, *especially* not the head of your company. But almost *everyone* likes to have a say in *some* decisions, especially the ones that affect them personally on the job every day—as long as they don't get in trouble for doing it."

"Yeah, I can see that," said Tom. "So, how do we do it?"

"Looking at the history of the quality movement can help you understand," replied David.

"Well, I've certainly studied that quite a bit lately," Tom mumbled.

"I know," David replied. Tom looked at him curiously.

"Ever since the quality movement started taking off in this country in the early 1980s, organizations have struggled with striking the right balance between unleashing the potential of the workforce and trying to maintain the discipline and control to keep things running predictably."

"You got that right!" agreed Tom. "We *still* have those debates on a regular basis."

"And it's going to continue until those 'opposing' forces see that they're not really on opposite sides of the fence," said David. "Here's how a lot people go at it. On one hand, you've got the *freedom fighters* who will continue denouncing control. They'll argue that traditional business methods in the US were trounced by other countries that adopted the people principles of quality gurus like Deming and Juran and Crosby. On the other side, the *commandos* will continue pushing for tighter constraints. And they'll point to evidence that the results of management methods like the late, lamented total quality management have been pretty dismal in most cases."

"So, how do you resolve the conflict and bring down those barriers and factions?" asked Tom.

"Remove the reason for fighting," replied David. "Truth is, neither of them is right—or wrong. Control is *not* a four-letter word ... and people will *never* give you their best effort with shackles around their hands and hearts and heads."

"Don't you think we've come a long way from the days of shackling people?" asked Tom with a tinge of sarcasm. "Seriously, I can tell you around here we really *want* employees to take initiative—to take some control, to give us their improvement ideas and help us boost performance. I know they have a lot of good ideas, and I think that a lot of other managers feel the same way."

"Are you getting the results you expected?" asked David.

"Obviously, it could be better," said Tom. "That's one reason we want to get this employee engagement plan in place. But one of our challenges is determining exactly what we can expect from people."

"Well, let me tell you something," replied David with a tone of caution. "No one deserves to get anything more than they expect out of life. That's true for organizations and individuals alike. So you'd better have pretty high expectations—especially if you want to win in the game of business. That includes your expectations for improvements from your employees. Frankly, they're ready to flood you with ideas—under the right conditions."

"You know, I really want to believe that," said Tom. "More than that—I *do* believe it—but we're not getting the kind of input from employees that you'd expect if that were true. So, what's getting in the way?"

"Well, let's start with the basics," David replied. "First, you have to demonstrate *unequivocally* how important their contributions are to the success of this company."

"Seriously, David, we've told employees how important they are more times and in more ways than I can count," said Tom.

"Listen carefully," said David. "I said you have to *demonstrate* the importance of their contributions, not *tell* them."

"Okay, I get what you're saying, but I think we've done that," said Tom. "So, tell me how *you* see the difference. How would you demonstrate their importance?"

"I'll start by giving you an example of what *won't* work, and see if it rings a bell," said David. "You start with a big kickoff meeting where you invite all employees and dispense the typical bromides about how much you value their ideas and suggestions. You serve up platitudes about how they're the most important asset in the organization, and tell them you know they have a lot more than just their hands to offer to the company. You express how much you value their brains and how you want them to make improvements that can make things better for the company and them, too. Sound familiar yet?"

Tom nodded and grimaced. He could picture the meeting room, the words and images on the projector screen, and the faces of the skeptical staff as they filed in to what he could see was a doomed start to another failed initiative. David continued.

"Then you top it off with a sugary coating of how deeply committed the management of the company is to supporting the new improvement effort, and you tell them you're going to give people big rewards for big ideas—the bigger, the better. You explain that you're setting up a new committee to review everyone's suggestions, and they're going to make sure the ideas get quick attention and a fair review. Then you tell your employees that the managers and supervisors are going to be expected to encourage and support employees in this program. If you haven't lost them by then, just use the E words. You know, tell employees you want to *empower* them and *engage* them—and just watch their eyes roll back in their heads."

"Again, I get your point," said Tom. "I'm reliving the employee eye roll as we speak. But I don't see anything wrong with trying to say the right things to people. We've been very sincere about it. The way you talk makes us sound pretty foolish."

"Not foolish—just *foolhardy*," replied David. "I'm not questioning the sincerity of what you've been saying to employees, but that's not enough. If your policies and systems and processes don't demonstrate the spirit of the words, you are definitely on a fool's errand. And like you said before, you've got smart, talented people here. You know they'll see through the charade by the time the meeting is over."

"I know we've tried to walk the talk," said Tom, "but for some reason, we're just not getting enough traction."

"Well, let's check out a couple of good indicators," said David. "I'm assuming you sit in on senior management meetings at least some of the time, right?" Tom nodded as David continued. "So where does the review of employee engagement in systematic continuous improvement appear on the meeting agenda?"

"Well, we sometimes have a status report on our major lean initiatives and Six Sigma projects," Tom replied. "Is that what you mean?"

"I doubt it," replied David. "If you're like most companies, only a small percentage of your employees typically get involved in those big projects. Also, people usually don't have much to say about whether or not they work on them—they just get assigned. What's more, big improvement projects can take people off the job for a long time—several days, even weeks sometimes. If that's what you're talking about, the answer is definitely no, that's *not* what I mean."

"Okay, so what *do* you mean?" Tom asked.

"Tell you what, Tom," said David. "I've got to take care of some other business right now, so let's pick up this conversation again a little later. And I want to ask you to do something before we get together next time."

"What's that?" asked Tom.

"I'm sure you've heard the old saying 'It's the little things that count,'" said David as Tom nodded. "I'd like you to think about why it's so popular—and why that idea is so important."

"That's all?" Tom asked. "What a relief! I thought maybe my next assignment was going to be watching *Sesame Street*."

"Not quite yet," David replied with a smile. "*Sesame Street* is pretty advanced stuff. We need to stick with the basics right now."

"You really know how to boost a guy's confidence," said Tom, grinning in return. "It's a bit humbling to think I'm not quite ready for Big Bird."

"I'm not concerned about your confidence," said David. "It's your complexity I'm trying to keep a lid on. Most corporate executives like you have a hard time remembering the KISS principle."

"You mean 'Keep it simple, stupid'?" asked Tom.

"No, I mean 'Keep it simple and *sincere*,'" replied David. "You know how cynical and cantankerous Oscar the Grouch can be. We can't have any of that if we're going to keep making progress."

"I'm beginning to think it means 'Keep it simple and *silly*,'" replied Tom wryly.

"That's very clever," said David approvingly. "See what a little imagination can do? Fact is, most executives would be a lot better off if they let themselves get a little silly once in a while."

"Oh, I think we get accused of that by our employees quite a bit already," said Tom.

"Don't confuse silly with stupid," replied David. "Employees don't mind a little silliness—in fact, it's healthy. It's when executives do things employees think are just plain dumb that they get nervous and critical."

"Touché," Tom replied. "Can I count on you to make sure I don't forget the difference?"

"I think you already know, Tom," David replied.

"How about this," Tom ventured. "If it's silly, it makes you smile, but if it's dumb, it makes you cringe?"

"Not bad," David said obviously pleased.

"Okay—simple, silly, and sincere," said Tom, grinning. "Wonderful words to live by, right?"

"Barney would be very proud," said David.

People want control and predictability, but they don't want to be controlled without having any say in the matter.

chapter 3
It's the Little Things That Count

As Tom walked into his office the next morning, the phone began to ring.

"Tom Payton," he said, as he picked up the receiver.

"Well, did you come up with anything?" asked the voice on the other end.

"David? Is that you?" replied Tom.

"Yeah, I wanted to make sure you did your homework," David said teasingly. "I've got some time right now if you want to pick up the conversation from yesterday."

"Love to," Tom replied. "I'll be right over."

As he walked out of his office, Tom was filled with an odd mixture of eagerness and curiosity. He wanted to know more about David and where he came from, but he didn't want to do anything to derail the conversations they were having. He liked what he was hearing, and he was enjoying the experience. For now, he decided, he would just go with the flow—and listen and learn.

As he walked into David's office, Tom noticed a penny on the floor.

"Hi, David," he said as he stooped to pick up the coin. "Looks like you lost a small treasure." He handed the penny to David.

"Thanks," David replied. "I'm curious—do you always pick up pennies when you see them on the ground?"

"I'm not sure," said Tom. "I suppose I do most of the time. Why do you ask?"

"You'd be surprised how many people wouldn't bother to pick up a penny on the street," said David. "Too much trouble. Just not worth it. Know what I mean?"

"Somehow I get the feeling this has something to do with what you asked me to think about yesterday," said Tom.

"Not very subtle, am I?" David replied, smiling.

"It's funny, David," said Tom. "When I got home last night, my five-year-old came running up to me all excited because his mother had just measured his height on the frame around the kitchen door. He's a bit obsessed about it right now, so we have lots of little marks that are just a hair's breadth apart from one another. Well, last night he was going wild because he's grown a quarter of an inch since the last time. You would've thought it was Christmas, the way he carried on."

"I think I hear a lesson from the proverbial mouths of babes coming on," said David.

"I've been thinking a lot since we talked yesterday," said Tom. "This whole business about the little things that count—it sounds so basic, almost trivial. I know it's important, but no one really takes it very seriously in the workplace. You know what I mean?"

"Sure do, and it's such a waste," David replied. "Fact is, most companies have some kind of process for working on the big things—just like the Six Sigma and lean projects you mentioned yesterday. Even though a lot of the improvement plans never get implemented very well, the intention and the effort are there. What's more, most people take them pretty seriously. But let me ask you this: What kind of impact would it have if every single employee was aware of—and took care of—all the little things that they have control over every single day?"

"It would be huge," said Tom.

"So why don't you track that kind of indicator on the senior management agenda at every meeting?" asked David.

"Well, a few things come to mind," Tom replied. "For starters, I'm not sure what it would look like or what we would discuss. It's also probably because it's hard to get excited about little improvements when you look at them one at a time. I guess another reason is that we don't have any effective way to capture and report on the little improvements or the impact they're having on overall performance. Is that what you mean? Stuff like that?"

"You're on the right track," said David, "so let's start with what it takes to get excited about the little things."

"Go for it," said Tom.

"First, you have to generate a lot of them," said David. He turned to the whiteboard hanging on the wall and started writing as he talked. "Like you said, no one is going to get very turned on by a few little improvements here and there. In order to get big numbers, here's what you have to do. You start by making the process simple and efficient, and then responding quickly to people's ideas. Then you need a reward structure that values all improvements equally—regardless of the size. And last, you have to give employees the responsibility and the support to implement their own improvements."

"I think we've done a pretty good job on some of those points," said Tom, looking at the bold words underlined on the board. "I mean, what could be simpler than filling out a suggestion form and submitting it for review and approval?"

"You have to be careful about this whole thing, Tom," replied David. "You can't just pick *one* of those key factors. It's all or nothing if you want to get results. Remember, I also said you have to respond quickly. How long does it take for a typical suggestion to make its way through your approval process?"

"It depends," replied Tom. "If it's relatively small and doesn't cost anything, it could get approved and implemented on the first go-around when our suggestion committee gets together at their monthly meetings. If it's complicated, or if it's going to cost a lot of money, it could take several more weeks or maybe months."

"That's where employee engagement stalls out in almost every organization," said David. "Listen to what you just said—it depends. First, if it's complicated and expensive, it's not a small improvement, right? Second, if it's taking you a month or longer to approve a small suggestion, how motivated do you think employees are going to be to participate? And how many improvements are you going to generate?"

"That seems pretty fast to me," replied Tom. "What's your idea of a rapid response?"

"How about ten minutes?" challenged David.

"I don't get it," said Tom. "Are you saying the committee has to be on call 24/7 and drop everything they're doing when someone has a suggestion?"

"No, I'm saying you shouldn't have a suggestion committee at all," David replied emphatically. "Certainly not for the thousands of little improvement opportunities that employees deal with every single day."

"Thousands?!" Tom exclaimed. "You've got to be kidding. There's no way we'd ever get that many improvement ideas from employees."

"Don't be so sure," said David. "Think about it, Tom—even on your own job. If you take a couple of minutes, you could probably name at least half a dozen things right now. You've dealt with them for years, and you've thought about fixing them. But you get wrapped up in getting the work out, and you don't ever give any serious attention to making the job easier or better."

"You're right," Tom agreed. "Instead of taking care of the root cause of the problem, I just work around it."

"It's like mowing the yard with dull blades," said David. "You know you could mow it faster and better if you'd take the time to get them sharpened, but you're just too busy, and you decide it's not really that big of a deal. After a while you don't even think about it anymore. You're stuck in a rut, and you just keep on mowing—a little less efficiently each time. That's the way it is with *every single employee* in every single job in your company, not just you."

"I know what you mean," said Tom. "But are you really serious about getting rid of the suggestion committee? We can't just let employees go around willy-nilly on their own, implementing whatever improvements they want, can we?"

"I agree," replied David. "That's what I meant earlier when I said you need some kind of control mechanism before you turn people loose with their imaginations. You need to understand that employees don't expect complete individual freedom and control."

"I'm not so sure about that," said Tom.

"Have you ever heard the line, 'Freedom's just another word for nothing left to lose?'"

"Okay, we're showing our age here, but yeah. It's from the song 'Me and Bobby McGee.'"

"That's right," David smiled. "You see, people understand that's what happens when everyone's free to do whatever they want no matter what. You get 'nothing left to lose.' They understand that unbridled freedom can lead to chaos and uncertainty. When it comes to the workplace, they want *some* control over their lives, not total control. For the most part, they're pretty happy to turn over the bulk of it to people they trust."

"Okay, so getting back to one of your other points, how do we make the improvement process quick and effective?" asked Tom.

"The answer lies more in the *who* than the *how*," David replied. "Who's the closest person with any management authority for frontline employees?"

"Their immediate supervisor," replied Tom. "But most of those folks aren't in a position to make decisions about improvements either without some type of review and approval process."

"And why is that?" asked David. "Before you answer, remember, I'm talking about the little things that are inside the scope of the work groups that the supervisors oversee. I'm assuming you've already got your lean and Six Sigma teams to deal with the big improvements. So why aren't supervisors in a position to approve the small improvements on their own?"

"Well, they are to some extent, I guess," replied Tom. "That's part of their job. But when I think of our supervisors and what they can do, we've got to keep some pretty tight limits on how far they take it."

"And why is that?" probed David.

"I guess it's because …" Tom paused while he tried to put his finger on the core issues. "Because we haven't given supervisors the authority and the skills they need to play that kind of role very effectively."

"Right on," said David. "I'm glad you acknowledged that the reason supervisors don't have what they need is more about shortcomings in the company's commitment to their development than anything about them personally. Too often, organizations just treat supervisors like hall monitors in school—you know, watching over the kids to make sure they do what they're supposed to do and don't break the rules. If that's how you think of supervisors, then that's what you're going to get. If you want more, if you want to accelerate employee engagement in making improvements, that's one of the first things you have to change."

"I have to be honest with you," said Tom. "It seems that supervisors are actually the ones who get in the way of employees submitting ideas. They seem to be a barrier more than a solution most of the time."

"That's true in a lot of organizations," said David. "But don't you think they're failing more because of what you said before? The need for them to have the right tools and authority more than any innate deficiencies they might have?"

"I think that's part of it," replied Tom. "But right now, I'm not sure they would do it even if they *did* have the skills and authority."

"Why not?" asked David.

"Mainly because they don't see it as an essential part of their job," Tom replied.

"Why not?" David persisted.

"Because *their* managers are telling them that they have other priorities," Tom responded. "Some of our managers put a lot of emphasis on getting the product out, and it's hard to get those managers to change their tune because *their* bosses on up the line are putting pressure on them, too."

"Sounds like the typical domino effect," said David. "But you told me a while ago that most of the managers really do value employee ideas. Why aren't they walking the talk?"

"It may go back to what you said earlier," Tom replied. "The number-one item on the senior management meeting agenda is production—not getting employees engaged in making improvements."

"Does that sound right to you?" asked David.

"To some extent," Tom replied. "But I really wonder, even if we did put it on the agenda, just how much we could get management to change their priorities—even the supervisors and frontline employees, for that matter. It's just not that easy to get people to change the way they think and act."

"That all depends on how compelling your vision and direction are," said David. "If you believe there's huge potential, and you put your money where your mouth is, people will eventually respond and adapt."

"I guess the bottom line comes down to actions and expectations," said Tom. "I can see the only way it's going to work is to get beyond the rhetoric. We have to make improvement part of what we eat, sleep, and breathe every day around here. Employees have heard all the ballyhoo and promises they can stand."

"Don't be too hard on yourself," said David sympathetically. "There's nothing wrong with the words—in fact, they're important. You just have to make sure you back them up with relevant action."

"So, tell me more about valuing all improvements equally, no matter what size they are," said Tom. "Why wouldn't we want to give bigger rewards for bigger or better ideas?"

"First of all, it takes you back to the committee again," said David. "If you don't have one, who else is going to decide which idea is worth $25 and which one is worth $250? That's especially problematic when there's no objective way to measure the financial impact an idea is likely to have. It forces your committee to make a subjective decision. Then employees start to think the committee is playing favorites when someone else's ideas get approved and theirs don't, or one gets a bigger reward than another one."

"Yeah, we run into that more often than I would like," Tom agreed.

"Even so, that's not the biggest problem with variable rewards," said David. "Think about human behavior for a minute. If you want to earn the big bucks—and who wouldn't, if that's how your incentives are structured—where would *you* focus your attention?"

"I'd go for the big ideas with the biggest payoff, of course," Tom replied. "But what's wrong with that? Isn't that what you want a program like this to do?"

"I don't know if you're much of a baseball fan," said David. "But if every player on the team came up to bat thinking he had to hit a home run, what kind of impact would that have on the team's overall batting average? What kind of value would they put on getting base hits? Don't get me wrong—home-run improvements aren't bad, and you have to have some power on the roster to knock one out of the park once in a while. But not many people can do that consistently, and you have to maximize the contribution of every single player if you want to win. What's more, baseball is a long-run game, just like business, and it's the little fundamentals that matter most over the course of an entire season."

"That makes sense," said Tom. "So, what do you do? Give the same reward to everyone who makes an improvement regardless of value?"

"Close, but not exactly," said David. "What you want to give is *equal opportunity* for earning equal rewards—regardless of how big the improvements are."

"What's the difference?" asked Tom.

"It goes back to baseball," said David. "You want everyone to get involved, even if they can't hit a home run. So you set up a periodic random drawing—once a week or every two weeks, even once a month can work—something fairly frequent. Then you enter employee names in the drawing for every implemented improvement they make during that time period. It doesn't matter how big it is or how much money it saves, they get one entry for every improvement that their supervisor has approved and they have implemented. Then you draw out a number of names, say, 10 percent of the total that have been entered, and you give the winners a small reward, something worth maybe fifty dollars or so. Just make sure it's not cash. Give them gift cards or a certificate for dinner and movie, something like that. People get weird when green stuff gets into the picture."

"Okay, but what about the other 90 percent?" asked Tom. "Aren't they going to be upset that we implemented their ideas and they didn't get anything for it?"

"Only if you believe the main reason people make improvements is because they want to win a prize," replied David. "But that's just not the case. I know it and you know it. The biggest motivation comes from someone showing gratitude for their initiative and respecting them enough to acknowledge the value of their ideas—and then doing something with them. What's more, *you* don't implement the idea in this process; the employee does—or at least they take responsibility for seeing it gets done with whatever help they may need. People get a lot of intrinsic satisfaction from doing that. It's just human nature."

"But I still think we've done that already," Tom argued.

"Maybe to some extent," said David with skepticism in his voice. "But here's the difference, Tom. Your current process doesn't say, 'We'll do whatever we can to support your initiative.' It says, 'Give us your suggestions, we'll run them through an evaluation process, and then we'll pick the ones we like and decide to implement.' The committee has the power, not the employees and their supervisors. It may work okay, but it won't light the spark for an explosion of employee improvements."

As he talked, David drew a flaming matchstick next to a wick on a barrel with the words *employee engagement* on the whiteboard. Tom thought he could almost see it flickering.

"I do see the difference," Tom acknowledged. "I can also see how a random drawing would cut down on the complaints about our suggestion committee making subjective decisions. And I can't blame the committee for it. They've got their own jobs to do, and it's a tough call sometimes."

"The drawing also adds some fun and celebration without making the rewards such a dominant part of the improvement process," said David. "It makes the incentives more like the spice in the soup instead of the stock."

"I like that," acknowledged Tom. "But can you tell me more about the other essential thing you mentioned for making this improvement program work—giving employees responsibility for implementing their own improvements?"

"First of all, don't ever call it a program," David said with a tone of warning. "When people hear the word *program*, they hear 'flavor of the month'—here today, gone tomorrow. It's important to treat improvement as an essential, integrated process that's woven into the basic fabric of the way you do business."

"I get what you're saying," said Tom. "That's why we have to make sure it's on the management meeting agendas, right?"

"Precisely," replied David. "Another way to shift from *program* to *process* is to be very clear that you expect every manager to make systematic improvement part of their essential duties and responsibilities. You do that by putting it in their job descriptions. If it's not there in very explicit terms, don't expect anyone to take you very seriously."

"So, is that how you make other employees responsible for their own improvements?" asked Tom. "Should we put it in their job descriptions, too?"

"That *sounds* logical, doesn't it?" David asked, clearly intending to go in another direction. "But I'm going to give you a different twist on how you get employees to take initiative. First, let me ask you something: If people are designed to use their imaginations—and let's assume they also want to be part of a winning team—why wouldn't they just make improvements without being coaxed and encouraged?"

"Lots of reasons," replied Tom. "I'm sure one of the big ones is that a lot of them have been told in the past to stick to their knitting. They've been directed to let the managers do the thinking about how to improve things."

"And sometimes employees just don't feel like it's worth the effort," David added. "They think no one will appreciate their idea, or worse yet, they might get in trouble if it doesn't turn out right."

David scribbled on the board: *ideas/good + mistakes/bad = no ideas.*

"As much as I hate to admit it, I know you're right," said Tom. "No matter how much we say we want people to take initiative, we always seem to find some way to shoot ourselves in the foot when they do it and they make some kind of mistake."

"Welcome to the club," said David sympathetically. "But none of the things you've mentioned begin to compare with the biggest stumbling block of all."

"What could be more discouraging than apathy or punishment?" asked Tom.

"I gave you a hint a little earlier," said David. "Remember when we talked about how we get overwhelmed with our work and get stuck in a rut? It's not just the workload that gets in the way of continuous improvement. The biggest problem is that we are creatures of *habit*. No matter how much work we have to do—or how little—we usually have some kind of process for doing things. Eventually, that process becomes a habit."

"But that's a good thing, isn't it?" questioned Tom. "Processes are part of the controls we need to do things consistently and produce predictable results."

"If they're designed and deployed right, processes definitely do lead to *predictable* results," replied David. "But that doesn't mean they're necessarily producing the *best* results or the results you need to beat the competition."

"We understand that," said Tom. "And we've got people looking at process improvement all the time."

"How many people?" asked David.

"Well, it depends on how you count them," replied Tom. "Like I said earlier, we have people assigned to big improvement projects most of the time, and our quality people are always looking at process issues. I don't know, maybe a couple hundred people at any point in time."

"Then you're missing out on the potential process improvements you could be getting from the other 19,800 employees," said David. "You see, every single job is a process, and those processes are made up lots of little sub-processes. That's true of almost every position, and every single one of them represents an opportunity to make things a little bit better or faster or cheaper or safer. Do you remember DJ's little growth marks?"

"Sure," Tom replied, eager to see where David was heading.

"He isn't going to grow into a full-grown man overnight," David continued. "It's going to come in little growth spurts that you measure day by day with those tiny marks on the kitchen doorway. Growth and improvement is almost inevitable if it's given the right environment."

"And it works the same way with employees in making improvements," Tom interrupted.

"That's right," David acknowledged. "The main reason employees aren't making those improvements is because they're stuck in the same rut and routine that most people experience in their daily work lives, and you're not making it easy or important enough for them to change it. The company is not providing the right nourishment to encourage growth, improvement, and change."

"Okay," said Tom. "So, how do we get them moving?"

"Create a different habit, a different *process* for breaking the habit of day-to-day routine," replied David.

Tom turned David's comment over in his mind for a while. Finally he replied, "It seems a bit ironic, doesn't it, that people are creatures of both habit *and* imagination?"

"Not really," David responded. "Remember when I said we are very similar to other animals in many ways. Animals are almost entirely creatures of habit. That's just about all they do. It's like the old song says: 'Fish gotta swim, and birds gotta fly.' But people have choices, and the way we exercise those choices—with our imagination and free will—is what makes us special, or at least different. Aside from that, we operate pretty much like every other living creature on this planet."

"When you put it like that, I guess it's not surprising that people just keep plugging along with their routines," Tom commented. "We really need to encourage them, and then we have to support them when they do make the effort to break out of cruise control."

"That's a nice analogy," David acknowledged. "Look at it closely, and you can see another problem with cruising along on the job. If you're going down the highway in cruise control, when do you get out of it?"

"Usually when I come up to traffic that's going slower than I am, and I have to hit the brakes," replied Tom.

"Just like most people," said David. "So, let me ask you this. How often do you *accelerate* when you're in cruise control—to make sure you don't lose any ground and you stay ahead of the 'competition' on the road?"

"Not nearly as often," replied Tom.

"I don't want to get too carried away with this example," said David. "For one thing, you've got speed limits to keep in mind when you're on the highway, but when it comes to business, there's no place for cruise control or speed limits. Not for a single employee—not if you want to win in the game of business."

"I know our management team feels that way, and we talk like that with our employees," said Tom. "But I don't know how well the message is sinking in."

"Remember, the conditions have to be right, Tom. It's not just about what you say," replied David. "What's more, people need time to adjust. You see, in some ways, we're really asking employees to act more like managers, to take charge of making improvements. They aren't used to thinking about themselves that way, and it takes a while to get them tuned in sometimes—even if they have the imagination and the will they need. So the way to get them on board is by encouraging them, coaching them on how to spot the little things they can control in their daily work processes, providing the support they need to make improvements, and giving them the responsibility and the time to implement them."

"I can see a couple of benefits from that approach," Tom remarked. "First of all, employees are more likely to identify opportunities that are genuinely important to them. And chances are better that they'll actually follow up on implementing their own ideas. They're also more likely to focus on the small things they can control—what you were saying earlier—the things that make their jobs more efficient day to day."

"There's another reason for stressing the importance of the small things—especially at the beginning of this process," said David. "Even in good companies, many people are afraid to take a chance and go outside the box to improve the way they do things." He pointed back to the words on the whiteboard—*no ideas*—and circled them. "But if the ideas are small, the downside risk is smaller, and people will be less hesitant to give it a shot."

"When you think about it, there's really no such thing as a small idea," Tom observed. "They're all important."

"You're partly right," said David. "A lot of ideas really are small, and that's a good thing, for all the reasons we've discussed. But no ideas are *insignificant*. That's really what you're trying to say, and you're absolutely right."

"And the more improvements they make, the more reinforcement they'll get," Tom continued. "And the more confident they'll become in doing it over and over again."

"That's right," said David. "It's really pretty basic. But I can't emphasize enough how important it is to do what you said earlier. You have to provide supervisors with the skills and the authority, along with the right expectations and support from *their* managers, if you want this process to get traction and produce big-time results."

"You're preaching to the choir on that point," Tom said.

"Yeah, and here's why it's so important," David continued. "For all of its power, imagination is also very delicate. You can crush it with something as small as a disapproving glance. I can't emphasize that enough. Supervisors need to understand that, and the entire management team from top to bottom needs to be on board in supporting them."

"That brings up another point," said Tom. "One of the biggest barriers for people is time. Even if everyone agreed that it's important to get all employees actively engaged in making continuous improvements, how do we fit that into the day? It's like you said about me earlier. I've got a lot of things that I'd like to do differently—better, faster, easier, whatever. But even if I tried to make a habit of it, I don't know where

I'd find the time to make improvements such a routine part of my workday."

"Habits have a way of taking care of themselves," said David. "That's why they're called habits. The real trick is getting over the hurdles to get *new ones* created. I know it can take a lot of motivation and rationale to change them sometimes, especially if the shift is a big one. But if the support is strong enough and the stakes are high enough, you can get it done. Once you convert to new habits, then the going gets a lot easier."

"I think we've got plenty of motivation and rationale," Tom said. "So how do we get over the hump?"

"I'm assuming you're planning to take these ideas to senior management at some point," said David. "When the question of time comes up—and it will—tell them to think about running the business like riding a bicycle. If you want to get the most out of the energy you're investing in it, you have to use both pedals. You need one to keep the day-to-day work running as smoothly and effectively as possible, and you need the other one for improving the way you do things every day. If you're only using one of those pedals, it's going to be choppy ride. It's also going to be slow, and you can be sure that someone's going to pass you up somewhere along the way."

"It's been a long time since I've been on a bike," said Tom. "But that's a pretty vivid image. I can see how exhausting and senseless it would be to use only one pedal. I think everyone else would see it, too, if I could find a way to get their attention. Maybe I ought to ride a bicycle to work wearing a Barney costume—what do you think?"

"I think you've had a little too much imagination to drink," David replied with a smile. "You'd better stay away from open windows for a while."

"Don't worry, David. I haven't lost touch with reality," said Tom returning the smile. "But I really do feel like I'm ready to fly."

Ideas/good + mistakes/bad = no ideas

chapter 4
The Truths and Realities about Human Beings

The view from Tom's office window was scenic enough for a postcard. The same was true of almost everyone else's office as well. Several years earlier, the company had decided to build its new corporate headquarters on the outskirts of the city. The campus stood near a wooded area that sloped down to the river winding its way through the region.

Despite its beauty, the scenery rarely captured Tom's attention anymore. He occasionally caught himself looking out the window while thinking about a problem, but his focus was seldom on the landscape. With his daily ritual of walking in and getting down to work, the view had become as commonplace as the furniture—except for this time of the year. On a clear day like today, in the middle of autumn, the sun reflected off the water and onto the wall of his office, creating a ripple effect that might've been compared to a cheap rotating landscape lampshade if it weren't for the novelty of this natural phenomenon.

As he looked back and forth from the wall to the window, Tom was struck by how this oddity illustrated David's point about the ruts that get created from daily routines. Without something to break everyday patterns, people are inevitably lulled into repetitive processes and behaviors that make them almost blind to opportunities for change and improvement.

As Tom reflected on the nature of that trap and how to avoid it, his thoughts began turning back to what David had said about the differences and similarities between human beings and animals—*other* animals, as David would put it. The similarities made sense: intelligence, the need for food, shelter, and even love and affection. But could the differences be as basic as free will and imagination? Even if they were, Tom had a lot of other questions about how to account for people's behavior in the workplace.

Suddenly, Tom found himself working his way almost unconsciously through the maze of hallways and cubicles to David's office. He was surprised at how eager he was to talk with David—and how pleased he was to find him at his desk.

"Hey, Tom," said David with genuine enthusiasm in his voice. "How goes the people business?"

"Funny you should ask," said Tom. "I was just thinking about the discussion we had the other day about people and animals, especially what makes us different."

"That usually throws people for a loop, but I wouldn't let yourself get too hung up on it," said David. "You see, what really matters is not what makes people different from other animals—it's understanding what makes people tick. It's knowing what lies at the heart of human nature, what drives the innate desire of people to give their personal best, and what gives them the ability to do it."

"But isn't human nature different from one person to the next?" asked Tom. "Isn't motivation different for every individual?"

"Those are two very different questions," said David. "You're right about motivation—that's going to vary quite a bit. But some things are pretty typical with everyone. You can see them in what I call the truths and realities about human nature in the workplace."

"Sounds intriguing," said Tom. "What are they?"

"Let's start with the basics. They're not very complicated, but they're important," said David. "Human beings have two essential needs: security and self-esteem. It's the simple man's version of Maslow's hierarchy, and it works just as well. The connection between those two needs and human performance is absolute. If people have self-esteem and security, they'll be inclined to perform well. If they don't, they won't. It's that simple."

"So how do security and self-esteem fit with imagination and free will?" asked Tom.

"Great question," David replied. "They really do go hand in hand. People need security and self-esteem to be on solid ground. But it takes imagination and free will for people to soar. When you've got them both in the right balance, that's when you get the best people have to offer. Think of it like a rocket ship. To get it off the ground and keep it moving, you need something to propel it. That's imagination and free will. To keep it from spinning out of control and crashing, you need something to keep it stable. That's security and self-esteem."

"I like that analogy—it makes a lot of sense," said Tom. "So what's next?"

"Here's my list of undeniable truths that apply to just about every person you'll ever know," said David, reaching into his drawer and pulling out a piece of paper.

Tom looked surprised as David handed it to him. He glanced at the paper and saw a list of points under the heading "Truths about People in the Workplace."

"Where did these come from?" asked Tom. "Wait … don't tell me. You imagined I was going to be coming by, and you knew I was going to need it, right?" Tom asked in a teasing voice.

"Not exactly," said David smiling. "It's all common sense. You know about these things, Tom. It's just easy to lose touch with them if you don't have a deliberate way to keep them alive every day."

Tom returned the smile and then read the list.

Truths about human nature in the workplace:

• *People want to do a good job.*

• *People want to be on a winning team.*

• *People want to be included and appreciated for their individual contributions.*

• *People have an innate desire to improve.*

• *People resist force and uncertainty more than they resist change.*

• *People assume greater responsibility when they are treated as adults.*

"Okay, these make sense. They ring true," said Tom. "But, tell me, why do you say they're undeniable?"

"Let's start at the top. People want to do a good job," David said. "I don't know if you've ever heard of a guy by the name of Douglas McGregor. What he said is a lot more famous than his name. In the early 1960s, he wrote a book called *The Human Side of Enterprise*. That book introduced the world to the notion of Theory X and Theory Y views of people in the workplace."

"You're right," replied Tom. "Just about everyone in the profession knows the terms, but I don't know many people who are familiar with McGregor's name. Your stock just went up another notch with me."

"I'll take that as a good thing," David replied appreciatively. "So as you know, Theory X says people are basically lazy and won't work unless they get pushed or threatened. Theory Y says people *want* to do a good job and they will—if they get clear direction and fair expectations along with the support they need to do their jobs well. Very few people would openly espouse a Theory X view of people in the work world today, but you'd never know it by the way some of them actually operate. Just look at the way systems and processes are designed to keep employees in line."

"But McGregor was right about Theory Y," Tom jumped in. "People really do want to do a good job, and contrary to what some managers think, no one comes to work saying I can't wait to get in and screw up today. It's just not human nature, to use your words. So what about your second point? 'People want to be on a winning team.'"

"It's pretty simple—yet quite remarkable—when you think about it," said David. "People love being part of a win. The reason that athletics are so hugely popular, especially team sports, is because people are so eager to be on a winning team. What's more, people will go a long way to help their team be a winner—as long as they get the right kind of support and encouragement."

"You know," said Tom, "when we talk about winning in this company, we really are talking about it mostly from a management and shareholder point of view. We spout the typical rhetoric that when the company wins, we all win. But I know we can make that message much more powerful and meaningful to people than we have up to now."

"It's also a very easy conversation to have as long as you get the message down to the grassroots," David added, "down to where employees can see clearly what's in it for them and everyone else when you win."

"So, tell me about the next point," said Tom. "It certainly doesn't take a brain surgeon to know that people want to be included and appreciated. You've talked about that already in the employee improvement process you described to me. Any other insights on that one?"

"You're right—it's not complicated. But it's important to emphasize it," said David. "Since people are naturally inclined to do a good job, they don't need a lot of special attention for a job well done. But no one likes to be ignored and kept in the dark either. An occasional pat on the back and maintaining open lines of communication can go a long way to making people feel like an integral part of the team. It helps them realize that you truly rely on them to make things work—"

"Like you said, though," Tom interrupted, "that's not hard to see, is it?"

"Often it's precisely because it's so simple that management often fails to put processes in place to ensure those open lines of communication are maintained systematically. That can lead to hurt feelings and resentment, which leads back to a lot of wasted time and hard work to reestablish the feeling of inclusion and appreciation."

"I can certainly appreciate that. Soothing ruffled feathers is not a very good use of any supervisor's time," Tom said, pausing a moment as he looked back at the list. "What about the next point, though? I guess it's pretty obvious, too, on some level. But I don't really see people demonstrating an innate desire to improve as much as I would expect," said Tom. "In fact, it seems that people tend to think about training and development as a requirement or a nuisance more than an opportunity."

"You need to look at it from a broader perspective," David encouraged. "If there's one thing you can count on with people, it's their desire to improve their lot in life. They want today to be better than yesterday, and they want tomorrow to be better than today. Of course, life doesn't show up that way all the time for any of us. It's a continuous series of ups and downs, and there's not much you can do about it. But just knowing that the desire for improvement is a common motivation for almost everyone is pretty exciting. It should make any organization salivate at the prospect of how that natural inclination can be translated into continuous improvement and innovation."

"I guess it's really a matter of tapping into a person's motivation—what inherently turns them on and where they want to see improvement—and then giving them what they need to get there," said Tom.

"I couldn't have said it better," replied David. "And it flows perfectly into the next point on the list: people resist force and uncertainty more than change."

"I like that distinction," said Tom. "But it flies in the face of what most people believe, doesn't it?"

"It makes me boil a bit whenever I hear someone say they can't make any progress at their company because people resist change," David replied. "People change all the time. Sure we all have our routines and preferences—the only ice cream I'll eat is rocky road—but without change, life would be pretty boring. You've heard the old saying 'Variety is the spice of life.'"

"It sounds like the same point you were making about people's need to balance control and predictability," Tom commented.

"Very similar," said David. "The truth is, most of the time when managers say that people resist change, what they're really saying is that they can't convince employees to do what they want them to do. I had to chuckle the other day when someone in another company asked me why he couldn't get employees to go along with an initiative he was trying to push with them. This will ring a bell for you. I asked him what it was and what his goals were. He told me it was a reengineering effort. He needed to reduce headcount, and he couldn't understand why people weren't eager to cooperate!"

"I hope you weren't too hard on him," Tom said with a knowing smile.

"It didn't really take much for him to see why he was having trouble in that situation," David replied. "But it's not always apparent to managers why they're not getting the response they'd like. Saying that people resist change is an easy out. People really don't resist change much at all. In fact, they like it—as long as it's not being forced on them, and as long as it's not creating more uncertainty about the future than they can handle."

"Makes sense," Tom agreed with a chuckle. "Reminds me of Dilbert and his pointy-haired boss with his harebrained ideas. You know, I don't think people really think those cartoons are funny—it's more like they're smiling with a wince because it's so similar to the nonsense they experience every day in their own jobs.

"Anyway, tell me about your next point," Tom said, turning back to the list. "People assume greater responsibility when they are treated as adults."

"Somewhere along the line, people got the misguided idea that managing was similar to parenting," said David. "Child rearing has changed a lot in the past thirty years, but it wasn't that long ago that the rule of thumb for kids was to be seen and not heard. They had to keep their noses out of other people's business, clean their plates, and head for the woodshed when they misbehaved. Kids hated it so much that they couldn't wait to grow up so no one could tell them what to do anymore. Then they got their first jobs, and look what happened?"

"I can see where this one is going," Tom replied.

"That's right," said David. "Their bosses tell them to do their jobs, not to bother management with harebrained ideas, keep their noses out of others people's business, and do what they're told if they don't want to get in trouble. It's subtler than it used to be, with all the emphasis on being politically correct these days, but it's still pretty prevalent.

"The main difference," he added with a chuckle, "is that managers don't make employees clean their plates! When organizations finally grasp the craziness of that approach—and they begin treating everyone in the workplace like a trustworthy, responsible adult human being— the impact on performance will be meteoric."

Tom felt a sense of clarity come over him, as though he was seeing an opening through a thick tangle of thoughts. He knew David was right, but he couldn't ignore his past experiences with employees who didn't behave like responsible adults.

David continued. "You see, Tom, if we all really understood and truly believed those things about people, we would run our organizations in very different ways. If we trusted the truths about human nature we've been talking about, we would do everything in our power to create workplaces that nurture those remarkable qualities and free them to flourish."

"That may be true for most people," said Tom with a tone of skepticism. "But I have to tell you, I know some folks who would never fit that model. They really come off like troublemakers, and if we freed them like you say we should, they'd flourish the business *right down the toilet.*"

"You can hold on to that belief if you want, Tom. But you pay a very dear price for it. For the sake of argument, let's assume you're right. Let's say 5 percent of the employees truly are bad apples. That means those truths *do* fit the other 95 percent of the people in the workplace. So here's the question that every organization has to ask itself. Do you want to design your operation to *defend* yourself against the 5 percent of the people that you call troublemakers? Or do you want to design it to *free* the potential of the 95 percent that come into work every day ready to give their best?"

"I get your point," Tom said.

"Here's a little reminder you can use when you feel yourself slipping back," David said. "Don't let a 5 percent problem get in the way of a

95 percent solution. Those truths may not fit everyone, but they cover the vast majority of people. What's more, they sure fit better than the principles and practices that most organizations use to deal with employees."

"I hear what you're saying," said Tom, "but honestly, David, isn't it more complicated than that? First of all, even though there are lots of similarities among people, there are also a lot of differences between them. And let's face it—people aren't perfect. Even the best of folks fall off the wagon sometimes."

"You're right," said David, reaching into his drawer once again. "So here's another list for you. I call this one the realities of people in the workplace."

Tom reached for the paper, smiling and wondering how David had more tips so conveniently available. On the page, he saw the following words:

Realities about people in the workplace:

• People view the world differently from one another.

• People have bad hair days sometimes.

• People make mistakes.

• People have old habits that die hard.

• People often don't have the skills to avoid and resolve conflicts.

"Now, these are employee traits I recognize!" Tom laughed. "If you've got the time, I'd love to hear how you deal with them."

"My time is your time," said David.

David's reply raised Tom's curiosity again. He was certainly glad to have the benefit of his counsel, but it made him wonder why David was willing to spend so much time helping him work through things.

"Great," Tom found himself saying quickly. "So how do you deal with these realities about people?"

"First, you have to set aside any judgment about them," said David. "And that's hard to do because they're more about the downside of people than the list of truths we just talked about. But they're just part of being human."

"Easier said than done, right?"

"Yeah, and it's really easy to use that defense when we're the ones behaving badly," David replied. "No one likes to admit messing up, so when we do, we say something like, 'I'm only human.' But we usually say it with a negative spin or some sense of resignation."

"You don't think we should feel good about messing up, do you?" Tom asked.

"Of course not," David replied. "But you hit it on the button a moment ago when you said people aren't perfect. That's not a *bad* thing in itself—it just is. It's only bad if you use it as an excuse to lay down and give up instead of picking yourself up and using those setbacks as a source of growth and aspiration."

"When I look at this list," Tom observed, "the first point about people viewing the world differently doesn't seem to imply anything negative at all. Why is it on here?"

"You're right," David acknowledged. "But it goes right to the heart of why we struggle making connections and working well with other people so often. We get caught in the mistaken belief that there's an absolute 'is-ness' in the world, that what we experience is what reality actually *is*."

"But it's hard for most people to look at it any other way," Tom said. "How do you get through to people with that idea?"

"Sometimes, I use a quote from the poet Anaïs Nin. She said, 'We don't see the world as it is. We see it as we are.' That's because all people come to their own perspectives in life based on their individual experiences. Since our experiences are never completely the same—no matter how much we share with other people—we're going to interpret and respond to events in our lives differently. So it's easy to see why it's so difficult to get hundreds or even thousands of people in a large organization aligned around common goals, let alone getting on the same frequency about how to achieve them."

"Easy to see, indeed," said Tom. "So tell me how we work around those different perspectives."

"That's for later," David replied, pointing to the list in Tom's hand. "For now, I just want you to get a clear picture of the nature of the realities on that list."

"Okay," Tom agreed. "So let's talk about bad hair days."

"Yeah, it's really just a continuation of the same thing we've been talking about," David said. "You commented a while ago that people all fall off the wagon sometimes. That's a fact, but it's only a problem if we choose to make it that way. It's just human nature. People slip a lot, and that can make life a real struggle sometimes. But we've got some pretty solid rules to live by that can help. We also have the ability to choose how we want to follow those rules, along with the awareness to sort through the consequences of our choices. Sometimes we make good choices. Sometimes we don't. We can either gripe and moan about it, or we can accept it as human nature and adjust for it."

"I guess it's easier to accept when you balance that reality with the truths you mentioned earlier," Tom commented.

"Absolutely," David agreed. "We'll talk more about that in a few minutes. First, let's finish the list."

"Okay, let's take an easy one," said Tom, scanning the list. "'People make mistakes.' No kidding, right? Isn't this similar to having a bad hair day?"

"Sort of," said David. "Let's take George as an example. He's a smart, dependable employee with a great attitude, but one day—a bad hair day—he slips getting into the shower and twists his knee. Then his car gets bumped from behind on the way to work, and he gets caught in a downpour before he reaches the building. On top of that, he's late for a presentation he's supposed to make."

"We've all been there at one time or another," Tom said.

"Wait, there's more," David continued. "Now, all that's bad enough, but to make matters worse, George also makes a mistake. He realizes that all his handouts are still on his desk—at home. Needless to say, he's not in a very good mood—and it shows."

"Well, I guess George can look at the bright side," Tom smirked. "Tomorrow really does have to be a better day."

"Do you think?" David replied. "Bottom line, even when we have every intention of doing the 'right thing,' even when we mean well, and we have a great attitude, and we have other people's interests at heart … life happens. The important thing is how we react to it—whether we beat up on people and punish them for those mistakes, or recognize their desire to do well and help them recover and get back on track."

"I have to admit that helping people recover is not one of our strong suits," said Tom. "We don't beat up on them, but the culture isn't as understanding and supportive as it should be either."

"The shame of it is that mistakes can really be great learning opportunities," David replied. "And not just for the person who made the mistake, but for everyone else who might be faced with a similar situation and who could learn how to avoid it."

"True enough," Tom agreed. "So tell me more about the next point: old habits die hard."

"This one can be really tough," said David. "Here you've got people who aren't intentionally misbehaving, who have made mistakes in the past, who want to get past their problems, but they just can't get rid of old habits that keep getting them in trouble. It can make life very difficult in the workplace, and overcoming it isn't easy sometimes. It takes a lot of patience and support to help people with this kind of problem. A little old-fashioned love and understanding helps, too."

"We also get impatient, and that blinds us to the possibility that people might be better suited to other jobs elsewhere in the company," Tom added. "Instead, we just let them go, and we lose a lot of the knowledge that those employees have accumulated over the years."

"You're right," David agreed. "What's more, that kind of move can be the perfect solution to two problems at once: getting someone out of a place where they're not suited and putting them in a position that you need to fill."

"So let's talk about the last one on your list—conflict resolution. That's a big issue, and we've actually done a fair amount of training in that area. But I'm eager to hear your thoughts about it."

"In a perfect world, people would have learned those skills a long time before they come to the workplace," said David. "We learn a lot of useful things in school, but for some reason they don't seem to teach much about how to deal well with conflict. If mistakes and misbehavior are part of human nature, we should learn very early how to avoid and resolve the inevitable conflicts they create. Unfortunately, most people don't have very good skills in that area, and that's why relationships can get pretty rough at work."

"And," Tom added, "that's why so many organizational development people like me spend a lot of time working with various departments to help them resolve their differences."

"Yes, but by then, it's often a case of too little too late," David said. "It would make your job a whole lot easier if people came to the workplace with a good understanding of the basic rules and tools for resolving conflict. But most don't, and that's why even well-intentioned people get into trouble sometimes."

"I can sure relate to that—along with almost everything else you've said about the realities of human nature," said Tom. "In fact, it looks to me like the realities, as you call them, are making the exact *opposite* point about people that you were making with your first list about the truths of human nature!"

"Maybe at first glance," said David. "But take another look. Do you notice anything about those realities that might make them seem not so contrary to the list of truths?"

Tom studied both lists for a moment. "Well, I guess one thing about the realities is that people don't really intend to do harm with any of them."

"Bingo," said David. "They're just gaps you have to contend with, and with some effort, most people can overcome whatever problems they might cause. What's more, you also have the wonderful truths about people to balance people's behavior. Those are powerful strengths you can build on."

"I hear what you're saying," said Tom. "The concepts all make perfect sense, but how do you build on them to create the right systems and processes for getting people tuned in, turned on, and equipped to play the game at the highest level possible?"

"Don't worry, Tom," said David. "I know the answers are fuzzy, and that can be pretty frustrating. The important thing to know is that you're knocking on the right door."

"That's encouraging," Tom said. "But it would sure be nice to get a better glimpse of what's on the other side of that door."

"I hear you knocking," said David. "The next time we get together, I'll see what I can do to answer the door for you."

People need security and self-esteem to be on solid ground. But it takes imagination and free will for people to soar.

chapter 5
Getting the Best Out of People

As Tom walked into the building, he found himself paying closer attention than usual to the beautifully designed entryway. He could spot the first-time visitors by the way they gazed around with admiring stares. It was a good example, Tom thought, of why organizations need a system to jolt employees out of their daily routines so they can see opportunities for continuous improvement in their everyday surroundings with fresh eyes.

As he headed for the elevator, he turned and glanced over at the receptionist in the center of the lobby. He could tell from the look on her face that she wasn't her usual cheerful self. Tom had hired her three years ago, and she had been great at her job from day one. She had a special gift for making everyone who came into the building feel at ease and worthy of her undivided attention. She truly was an outstanding asset to the company, and the two of them had developed a warm relationship.

"How are things going, Mary?" asked Tom.

"Oh, they're okay, I guess," replied Mary unconvincingly.

"Well, you'd better tell your face about it," said Tom teasingly.

"Sorry, Tom," Mary replied with a bit of a smile. "The truth is, my boss just told me that I have to work on some reports when I'm not greeting people who come in the door. You know we get a pretty steady flow in here sometimes, and I get such a charge out of making people feel welcome. It may sound corny, but this is such a great space, and I really love what I do. Don't get me wrong—I don't mind doing the extra work, but I don't know how I can concentrate on doing both jobs well."

"I didn't know about that," replied Tom sympathetically. "Do you think maybe there's some way things can be arranged so you can do both jobs in a way that works for you?"

"I'm not sure," Mary replied. "But thanks for asking. I appreciate it."

"Think about it, and let's talk about it later," said Tom.

As he walked to the elevator, Tom reflected on the truths and realities about people that he and David had discussed the day before. He had a feeling that something was missing from their conversation. Just as he was about to walk into his office, he saw David coming down the hall.

"How come you always seem to show up when I'm puzzling over some kind of people problem?" asked Tom.

"Lucky, I guess," replied David. "What's going on?"

"Have a seat, and I'll tell you about it," Tom replied, taking off his jacket and hanging it on the back of a chair. "I just ran into a pretty unhappy employee, our receptionist. It seems her boss gave her some new job duties, and she's concerned about how it's going to affect her performance."

"You can probably hear the source of the problem already in the way you described it," said David.

"Do you mean when I said he *gave* her the job duties?" asked Tom.

David nodded as Tom continued. "I get that, but the fact is, sometimes a manager really does need to have people do certain things, and it's not always going to be something people like. How do you do that in a way that doesn't turn someone like Mary sour on her job?"

"We already talked about some of the things you need to do in that kind of situation," replied David. "It's partly rooted in needing to strike that delicate balance between freedom and control—or more to the point, between freedom and *being controlled*."

"I can hear where you're going," said Tom.

"I'm sure you can, and here's a question for you," said David. "How many times have you heard a manager complain that she can't figure out how to motivate her people?"

"You mean other than me?" Tom replied with a grin.

"It's pretty common, isn't it?" said David. "So here's the first thing I tell people when they ask me that question. Unless you've taken in slaves or God has taken you in as a partner, they are not *your* people. They are independent, competent adults who expect to be considered with respect, and they will respond negatively if they are treated like children or chattel."

"I think I'm beginning to see a theme here," Tom commented. "So, what's the second thing you tell them?"

"It goes back to something else we discussed before," replied David. "You can't motivate other people. Fortunately, though, motivation is intrinsic. Human beings are endowed with all the motivation they need in life. If you want to optimize it, you need to tune in to the unique individual spark that lives within each and every person's soul. Then you have to watch out for the barriers that can put out that spark, and remove them so people's natural motivation can flourish."

"Another familiar thread," Tom commented. "What else?"

"I tell them one more thing," David replied. "Most managers are not really trying to motivate people. They're trying to figure out how to get employees to do what they want them to do, even if the employees don't want to do it."

"That's basically what's happening with Mary," Tom replied. "And part of it, I'm sure, comes down to the way her boss told her about her new job duties."

"You're right, but like you said, that's just part of it," replied David. "The words that managers use and the actions they take are a direct reflection of how they think about their jobs. If it's about using employees so the manager can get his job done, that kind of egocentric view is doomed to failure from the start. Partly, it will fail because it assumes that managers have more important work to do. It also suggests that managers have the best answers. If there's one clear lesson that the quality movement has taught us, it's this: Every single *body* in the workplace also comes equipped with a *brain*. Any organization that fails to take full advantage of both muscle and mind from everyone on the job is diminishing its potential for exceptional performance."

"True enough," said Tom. "So after you give managers a good tongue-lashing, what's next?"

"I tell them to ask a different question," David replied. "Instead of asking how to motivate people, they should ask themselves 'How can I get the best that people are *able* and *eager* to contribute to the success of this organization?' That's more relevant to the truths and realities of people. It also provides the foundation for a process I've developed to get people tuned in to what managers need to get done. Bottom line, if you want to get the best out of people, help them focus on *what they do best naturally.*"

"What's the chance you're going to reach into your desk drawer and pull out another list?" asked Tom with anticipation.

"Pretty good, actually," replied David.

Tom reached out to take the sheet of paper that David held out to him. The top of the page read,

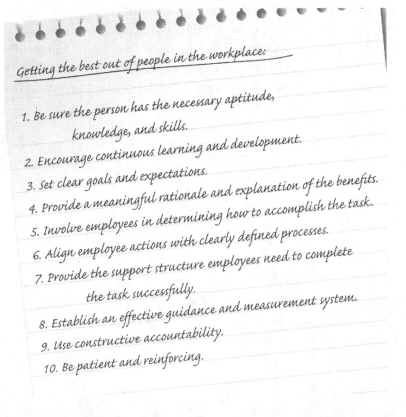

Getting the best out of people in the workplace:

1. Be sure the person has the necessary aptitude, knowledge, and skills.
2. Encourage continuous learning and development.
3. Set clear goals and expectations.
4. Provide a meaningful rationale and explanation of the benefits.
5. Involve employees in determining how to accomplish the task.
6. Align employee actions with clearly defined processes.
7. Provide the support structure employees need to complete the task successfully.
8. Establish an effective guidance and measurement system.
9. Use constructive accountability.
10. Be patient and reinforcing.

"Looks pretty complete," said Tom. "The whole business about making sure that people have the right skills sounds like a good place to start."

"Don't forget aptitude," David jumped in. "That's really where you have to begin. Aptitude is an intrinsic quality. Skills and knowledge are acquired. When it comes to *aptitude*, it's important to make sure that you're not trying to put a square peg in a round hole."

"We really do try to make sure that we make a good match between a person and the job—at least initially," Tom replied. "But when they don't perform well, we tend to see it as a failure of the employee, and sometimes we don't make a strong enough effort to look for a better match."

"You're not alone," said David. "I emphasize the point sometimes with an old joke I heard a long time ago. You know why you shouldn't try to teach a pig how to sing, don't you?"

"Why's that?" Tom asked, playing along.

"First of all, it doesn't work," David replied. "Second, it makes the pig madder than hell."

"Sort of reminds me of when I was a kid trying to learn how to play the trumpet," Tom replied through his laughter. "I didn't really get mad, but no matter how hard I tried, I just couldn't get the hang of it. I got really frustrated, and I felt bad because I couldn't keep up with the other kids in the school band."

"So you can really appreciate the aptitude factor," David said. "When you've got that one figured out, then and only then do you turn to developing skills and knowledge. That process is pretty basic. You start by assessing what the gaps are between where people are and where they want to be, and then you set up appropriate learning and development plans tailored for each person. Of course, those plans should be based on both what the organization needs from that employee and what that person aspires to do within the organization."

"Okay, so tell me about the next item on your list," said Tom. "Goals and expectations—sounds pretty obvious to me."

"And there's the rub," David replied. "Most of these guidelines are pretty basic on the surface, but it's surprising how poorly many managers and supervisors put them into practice. They give employees some vague sense of what they want them to accomplish, or maybe they just send them out onto the field without even telling them where the goal line is. It's like playing a soccer game and your team doesn't know where the goal is, or a basketball game where they can't find the basket."

"Pretty hard to score points that way," quipped Tom.

"Indeed, and it's a sure formula for failure," David continued. "You have to give people a clear line of sight to where you're heading, what you expect of them, and what their responsibilities are—for both specific situations and overall duties. Otherwise, there's a real good chance they won't meet your expectations. The more specific you are with goals and expectations, the more likely it is that you'll achieve the desired outcome."

"It really comes down to good old effective communication," Tom said. "We offer managers and supervisors training to help them connect better with employees, but I think it needs a lot more reinforcement than we give it. So tell me about the next one, 'rationale and benefits.'"

"Be sure to add the word *meaningful* to that one," David said. "When you tell people to do something, they are likely to have a couple of basic questions: Why should I do it? What's in it for me? It's a personal thing, and how you respond will determine how much buy-in you get. If the only reason people do things is because they are being told to do them, they won't bring their best effort and energy to the task. They're also more likely to badmouth it when they talk with other employees. You have to explain why it's important, and you have to make it a win-win proposition."

"I'll buy that," said Tom. "So let's talk about the next point— involving employees in determining how to accomplish the task they're assigned. That's probably the main place where Mary's boss went wrong."

"That's at least part of it," agreed David. "If Mary is as good at her job as you say, she's probably knows how to get his reports done and still stay on top of her receptionist duties."

"I'm sure that's true," Tom replied. "And he'd be the first to agree. He knows how good she is; in fact, that's probably why he thought it wouldn't be a problem to give her the additional workload. But you're right. He didn't ask for her ideas, and instead just assumed she could get it done. When you just dump on people—even good people—you're missing out on their ideas, and you can turn them sour on their jobs."

"Let's talk about the need for well-defined processes," David continued. "Even if you get people effectively engaged and they're clear on where they're heading, they may struggle with how to carry their jobs out if they don't have clearly defined processes for doing what they're supposed to do. That's particularly true if it's something they don't do every day—and even more so if it involves working with people from other departments."

"Who should create those processes?" asked Tom.

"It depends," David replied. "Obviously, supervisors and managers have to play a part, but if the employees involved in the process can weigh in on it, so much the better. Regardless of who does it, though, people need clearly defined processes to follow—sort of like an instruction manual—if you want consistent execution of the tasks you assign to them."

"So what about support structures?" asked Tom. "How are they different from processes?"

"Processes are like a road map," David replied. "Support structures are the things you need to help you make the journey: the car, the gas station, even the road itself."

"I get the difference," Tom said. "Tell me more."

"Even if people know the goal, what's expected of them, and the processes for getting there, they probably won't perform well if they don't have the support they need," said David. "On the job, that support might include resources, funding, people, communication tools, a healthy working environment, managers endorsing their work, supervisors clearing obstacles—a long list of things."

"And it's logical that people are more likely to perform the way you want if they get the support they need," said Tom. "I'm curious about the next one on your list, though. What does establishing an effective guidance system look like?"

"That's one of my favorites," David replied. "It's quite simple, actually. It's also vitally important, yet it's so often overlooked."

"I'm all ears," said Tom.

"Getting where you want to go—or where you're supposed to go—takes some tools to make sure you stay on the right path," said David.

"First, people need measures. If you want them to accomplish a certain task with specific outcomes within a given period of time, they need explicit information about those expectations. Then they need some type of communication process to let them know on a regular basis if they are on target or not."

"It sounds like the balanced scorecard we use," said Tom.

"You're right, but that's only half of it," said David. "It's important that you don't take the communication part for granted. It needs to be frequent and systematic—not just an occasional casual review or an end-game tally of the final score."

"Otherwise, you won't know if you're on course to win the game along the way," said Tom.

"Absolutely," replied David. "And that's why you also need a systematic, preset mechanism for taking corrective action if you're off course. Some people call it 'scenario planning,' and the rationale is simple. If you wait until you hit a roadblock before you decide how to overcome it, your response will be slower, and the results will be less effective."

"We try to do that at the corporate level," said Tom. "It only makes sense that it should work at the individual level, too. So tell me about the next one on the list, constructive accountability. That has a nice ring to it."

"Of all the people-related terms that you hear knocked around in organizations these days, accountability is probably the most misused and misguided of them all," said David. "The first mistake is that people use *accountability* and *responsibility* as interchangeable terms. They're related, but quite distinct. Responsibility means you're in charge, and whether or not it gets done is up to you. Accountability is about consequences—good ones if you fulfill your responsibility, and not so good ones if you don't. And that's up to someone else."

"That really is an important distinction," said Tom. "And you're right —I don't think many people really appreciate the difference."

"If you want to get it right, you have to be especially careful about the verbs you use with those two words," David added. "When it comes to responsibility, for example, that's something you *give* to people. When it comes to accountability, though, that's something you *hold* people to. They can accept or decline responsibility, but once they do that, they don't have a choice about accountability. That comes with the territory, and it's controlled by the person you made the agreement with to accept the responsibility."

"I can just see myself trying to get people to change the way they use those terms," said Tom with a chuckle of resignation.

"I wouldn't lose any sleep over it," said David. "What's more important is how to handle accountability in a constructive way. Truth is, most responsible adults have no problem with being held accountable for their actions. People actually thrive in environments with appropriate accountability. But if the only tools you have for holding people accountable are punishment and criticism, you will never get the best performance out of them."

"I totally agree," said Tom. "But in the heat of the moment, when you've got a problem, it's easy to slip into a negative reaction. How do you control that?"

"You have to start by assuming that most people want to do a good job, like we discussed earlier. Not just once in a while, but all the time," David replied. "Then there's one thing you should do every time you're facing a performance problem."

"What's that?" Tom asked.

"If you never remember another thing I say, tuck this away where you'll never forget it," said David.

"I hope the payoff is as good as the setup," Tom said with a smile.

"Always approach people as the *source of the solution,* not the *cause of the problem.*"

"Hmm … I like that a lot," Tom said, turning it over in his mind.

"Why do you think that's so important?" David asked.

"Quite a few things come to mind," said Tom. "First of all, people won't be so defensive, and they're less likely to bring up a bunch of excuses. They'll also feel that you care more about helping them fix the problem than taking them to task for messing up. And one more thing—you're giving them the responsibility to fix the situation."

"You keep that up, and I'm going to start coming to *you* for advice instead of the other way around," said David.

"Thanks," said Tom. "But it's pretty easy to see when you think about how people tend to react to criticism."

"Sometimes, the easier things are, the harder they are to see," said David. "So, are you ready for the last point about being patient and reinforcing?"

"Bring it on," Tom replied. "Lord knows, we can all use some help when it comes to patience and reinforcement."

"It's hard to do sometimes, I know, especially in a big, fast-paced company like this one," said David. "Fact is, though, sometimes people just don't seem to get it. No matter how many times we guide them, support them, and instruct them on how to do something differently, they fall back into old familiar patterns of behavior."

"Isn't that what you meant earlier about trying to put a round peg in a square hole?" asked Tom.

"Not really," David replied. "Sometimes the fit is fine, but it just takes a while to get things to click. You know as well as I do that changing old habits is not easy for most people. It takes a lot of repetition before they get comfortable with it, and they need support and encouragement when they get off track. But as long as there is a genuine willingness to improve—and if the aptitude is there—patience and reinforcement usually pay off in the long run."

"I think we all know it takes time for most people to get adjusted to something new," agreed Tom, "but when the pressure is on to perform every minute of the day, we aren't very good at cutting people much slack sometimes. Still, sometimes I wish people were more thick skinned when a manager doesn't use the most ideal communication style in telling an employee to do something."

"The thickness of people's skin has nothing to do with it," said David. "The issue has *everything* to do with where we started our whole conversation—the unique capacity that people have for imagination, and the free will they have to empower it. That's the reason people hate having to toe the line like robots or step like drones to the beat of the corporate drum. If that's what you want people to do, then you need to talk with someone else because I can't help you."

"Like I said earlier, I really am a Theory Y sort of guy," Tom replied a bit defensively. "But surely you can understand getting frustrated at how tough it can be to deal with people sometimes."

"All right, since you mentioned the word *deal*, I'm going to give you one more way to get people on board with what you need them to do in an organization," said David. "You can put just about all types of job-related activity into three categories: play, work, and hell."

"I don't know about the play part, but I'm sure most employees would agree with the other two," said Tom.

"So tell me, what do you think of when you hear the word *play*?"

"Having fun … doing something you enjoy … having a good time … goofing around—stuff like that," Tom replied.

"Do you ever associate any of those words with what people do on the job?" asked David.

"Not really … except maybe goofing around once in a while," Tom replied.

"So here's how it translates into what people do on their jobs," said David. "*Play* is what they are willing to do just because they love doing it. If they actually make a living at it, too, that's a bonus. In fact, they even feel guilty about it sometimes. They can't believe that someone is willing to pay them to do something they love so much. It's real work, but it's also real fun. That's what I call play, and you rarely have trouble getting people to do those kinds of things on the job."

"I can buy that," Tom agreed. "But I don't think you're going to find too many people who feel that way about their jobs in most organizations."

"What about Mary?" asked David. "Sounds like that's how she felt about her job until her boss threw a monkey wrench into it."

"Touché," said Tom. "So, tell me about work and hell."

"Work is what makes up most of what people do on the job," said David. "They don't mind doing it—in fact, it's what they expected when they took their jobs. They probably find it agreeable most of the time, even satisfying as long as they don't run into some kind of trouble with it. Still, they expect to be paid for it, and they won't do it if they aren't. That's why pay is called compensation."

"Okay, I get that one," said Tom. "Tell me about hell."

"It's just what it sounds like," said David. "Hell is what nobody wants to do, and you probably can't pay them enough to do it—at least not willingly. For that stuff, you have to say 'Let's make a deal,' and that's exactly what you do."

"So what kind of deal are you talking about?" asked Tom.

"Let's take Mary again," David replied. "I don't know if she would call her situation hell exactly, but it's clearly not part of what she expected when she took the receptionist job."

"And she's definitely not feeling very good about it," Tom added.

"That's right," said David. "Now if her boss had sized up the situation a little differently, he could've started by asking Mary how she felt about taking on the extra duties. After she told him about her concerns, he could've acknowledged her in two ways. First, he could ask her to help him figure out how to make it work. He also could've said, 'Okay, Mary, I see the problem. But I really need your help on this. What kind of a deal can we make? If you do this for me, what can I do for you?' See what I mean?"

"I can see that kind of approach working in some situations," Tom replied. "But I have to admit it seems like an odd way to work with people."

"So, how does it compare with the frustrations you have in dealing with them when you shove stuff down their throats that they don't like?" asked David.

"Point taken," Tom acknowledged.

"I know it's not easy, Tom," said David. "But let me warn you, if it ever gets smooth and easy with people, then you've got a lot more to worry about than your frustrations. There's a fine line between smooth and stagnant. Sometimes smooth sailing is a sign that people have put their imaginations in park and their performance on cruise control. When that happens, you'll never get the best out of people because you can't force imagination. You can only create the right conditions for it to thrive, and one of those conditions is supporting people in the pursuit of their own motivations."

Tom peered out the window, deep in thought. "Well, I can see I need to do a couple of things," said Tom. "First, I need to have that talk with Mary. It's incredible how we trip up when we get more focused on the task instead of the people who have to do it."

"That's for sure—even if we don't mean to do any harm," David added. "So what's the second thing?"

"When you said we have to support people in pursuit of their own motivations, it made me think about employee development and all the stuff that goes with it—like performance appraisals," said Tom.

"I've got one scheduled tomorrow, and it could be a tough one. I'm not looking forward to it, and I know there's got to be a better way to do these things. I'm determined to develop a better process, and I know it's going to take some new thinking. Can I count on you to give me some coaching on it?"

"You know where to reach me," David replied.

"Oddly enough, *you* always seem to find *me* just when I need some advice."

"Like I said before, my time is your time," answered David.

"Any parting words for me to ponder before we talk about it?" asked Tom.

"Just ask yourself a question," David replied. "How often do you hear managers saying how much they enjoy giving performance appraisals, and how often do you hear employees raving about how much they love getting them?"

"Uh, let's see ... never and never."

"So, think about why performance appraisals are such a problem."

"Any chance it has something to do with imagination and free will?" asked Tom with a knowing smile.

"You really had to reach for that one, didn't you?" asked David jokingly. "Enjoy the humor while you can. Tomorrow's conversation is going to be a little rough for you."

Tom's smile masked his anxiety. Figuring out how to develop a really great performance appraisal process was one of his biggest challenges, and he was pretty sure David was going to drill him on it.

"I'll be sure to wear my big-boy pants," Tom said jokingly with a half-hearted smile.

Always approach people as the source of the solution, not the cause of the problem.

chapter 6
Focusing on Development
Instead of Appraisal

Tom was more than a little eager to talk with David. He had just finished the performance appraisal they had talked about yesterday—and it had not gone well. He reached for the phone to give David a call, but he realized he didn't know how to reach him. He put the phone down and swiveled in his chair to look out the window. He was trying to relax, closing his eyes to reflect on what had gone wrong. After a few moments, he heard David's voice snapping him back to the present.

"You look like your worst enemy just won the lottery."

"No, I'd eventually get over that," replied Tom, only mildly surprised at David showing up at precisely the right time. "I just came out of a performance appraisal session with someone who reports to me. Do you remember what you told me about all job activity being play, work, or hell?"

"Let me guess," said David. "This one produced a lot of heat, right?"

"You got that straight," Tom replied.

"Looks like perfect timing," David replied. "I know you wanted to talk about development and appraisal anyway. What happened with this guy?"

"Like you said, it's pretty much the same thing that happens when people don't get what they expect," replied Tom. "We talked about his performance during the past year—you know, the good, the bad, and the ugly. Then I gave him a rating of three on our five-point scale, and he got very upset. I can sympathize with the guy. He's a hard worker, but the truth is, he's just an average performer. I don't think it's fair to everyone else to rate him any higher than a three. Besides, I've only got so much money to spread around for salary increases, and I have to save a sizable chunk for my superstars."

"Their agents must be pushing a pretty hard bargain this year, eh?" said David with a smile on his face.

Tom flashed a quick grin back, but he wasn't in the mood for joking around.

"Seriously, David," he answered, "performance appraisal is one of the most frustrating processes I've ever had to manage as an HR professional. Most people, except those who get the highest ratings, think they should have been rated higher, and the superstars think they should get more money for their exceptional performance. You can't win for losin'.'"

"So, why don't you get rid of it?" asked David.

"Here we go again," Tom replied with a feigned tone of resignation. "You've just about got me sold on getting rid of the suggestion committee, but surely you aren't serious about performance appraisal. How would we evaluate people and decide on raises? Just have everyone spin the wheel of fortune?"

"That would certainly be more objective," David replied. "I talk with a lot of companies about performance appraisal. When I do, I always ask them if the majority of the employees like getting it and the majority of their supervisors like giving it. What percent of those companies do you think answer yes?"

"Probably none of them, if they're being honest with themselves," replied Tom.

"I typically find it's between 10 and 20 percent," said David. "But I agree with you that there's probably some wishful thinking in most of those cases. So, here you have a process that employees hate, supervisors avoid, and HR people like you get frustrated over. Why in the world would you want to continue doing something like that?"

"You've got to have some kind of system to let people know how they're doing," Tom replied. "And we need some kind of mechanism to keep our compensation system in balance."

"Let's go back a few years—actually, quite a few years," said David. "Back to when you were in first grade. Do you remember your first report card?"

"I can barely remember the grades I got in college," Tom replied with a wave of his hand.

"I don't mean the grades," said David. "Do you remember how you *felt* when you got that first report card?"

"Not specifically in first grade," Tom replied. "But as far back as I can remember, I know that I liked getting the good grades ... and I didn't like the bad ones. How's that for a blinding flash of the obvious?"

"Yep, and guess what?" said David. "That's the truth about all people—no matter what age they are—and regardless of whether it's at school or at work."

"But when you get right down to it, isn't all of life kind of a performance appraisal process?" asked Tom. "When you do well, you get rewarded—you win somehow. When you don't do well, you lose. And when you do *really* badly, you get punished, especially if it's intentional. That's just life."

"Sounds pretty grim for everyone except the winners, don't you think?" asked David. "Let's come at it from a little different slant. In a perfect world, what's the purpose of education?"

"Gee, I think I should be able to get this one right," Tom replied. "Would it be to learn the things you need to know to get along in life?"

"And how do most people feel about learning?"

"I think most people like to learn," said Tom. "It's just school they don't like," he added with a grin.

"Sad but true," David continued. "And there are all kinds of reasons why kids don't like school that have nothing to do with report cards. But one thing is clear. People enjoy learning most when they have some control over what they're learning and how they're doing it. That's also when they typically learn *best*, especially as people get older."

"It sounds like what we were discussing earlier," said Tom. "When you're a kid, you're pretty used to having people tell you what to do. Then you get into the workplace, and all of a sudden, there it is all over again. People are telling you what to do and how to do it—and then every year someone's grading your performance. It's like being a kid all over again."

"Exactly," said David. "But now, it's not just grades. It's money, career choices, lifestyle. A lot depends on those 'grades' when you're an adult."

"I hear what you're saying," said Tom. "But what's the alternative?"

"If the purpose of education is learning, you don't need a report card to tell you how you're performing," said David. "A good teacher knows how well a student is doing, and she knows what kind of help and direction the student needs without giving a score. Report cards and test scores are to let everyone else know how students are doing, not to enhance the learning experience. No one ever learned anything from a test or a report card."

"That may be true," said Tom. "But what's wrong with letting people know how students are stacking up to other kids in their class, and how they compare to other schools?"

"I see it as a necessary evil when it comes to schools," said David, "but it's a complete fallacy in the workplace."

"How's that?" asked Tom.

"How many companies have you ever seen compare employee grades and test scores with the competition?" asked David. "The fact is, in virtually every company, employees are graded on a comparative basis with their own coworkers. And in most of those companies, there's a somewhat skewed distribution of grades over the classic bell curve. In your system, for example, a few people would get 5s and 2s. Most would get 3s and 4s. And no one ever gets a 1—otherwise, they'd be long gone. Sound about right?"

"Close enough," Tom replied.

"So let me ask you this question," said David. "How does all that help you be more competitive? From what I can see, the only competition in that kind of system is among your own employees. And if it's tied to compensation, what's the incentive for your superstars, as you call them, to help the people with lower grades to improve their skills and performance? It just makes it harder for them to differentiate themselves and keep getting bigger raises than their coworkers."

"I have to confess," said Tom. "We've been trying to figure out how to take greater advantage of our star performers. We wanted them to do some mentoring with their teammates, but it hasn't really gotten much traction. I can see why to some extent. Still, if you're a stand-up employee, and if you're committed to the company and the well-being of everyone on the team, I'd expect you to step up and do whatever you can to help other people out, wouldn't you?"

"Get real, Tom," David said. "Sure, they want the team to succeed, and they'll be happy to do almost anything they can to ensure that success—but not if it's going to hurt their own wallets. In a zero-sum game like that, the only way to win is for someone else to lose. And the only way to avoid that trap is if helping one another increases the payout for *everyone.*"

"Okay, I get the idea," said Tom. "I'm not sure how to make it work yet, and I want to come back and talk more about it later. Help me out, though, because a lightbulb went on for me when I said that people really do love to learn. I know some top companies have done a great job with employee development, but we just haven't kept pace. What does it take to get people motivated to do it?"

"If you really believe what you said about people loving to learn, then you'll understand that you don't have to motivate them," said David. "Most people already have all the motivation they need. You just need to provide the right support—things like tuition reimbursement, access to information on what development programs are available, advancement opportunities, and other things like that. You also need to customize the learning with each employee so you're providing them with what that they find personally relevant and enjoyable."

"We get that," said Tom. "But it's a real challenge. There's a lot of stuff employees *have* to learn on top of what they *want* to learn. People are jammed with work, and there's only so much time in the day."

"I'm seeing more and more of that with companies that are trying to get mean and lean, and I understand what's driving it," David acknowledged. "But if people sacrifice development so they can get the work out, the consequences are inevitable. You're going to wind up losing the game in the long run. You've heard of Ken Blanchard, right?"

"Sure, he wrote *The One-Minute Manager* a long time ago."

"He's done a lot more since then, but yeah, that's the guy," David replied. "He says that growth and development are like oxygen to a deep-sea diver. If you can really get your head around that analogy, it's pretty rich. When you shortchange your development efforts, people start gasping for air. Eventually, they might even suffocate. When that happens, everyone loses—the employee, the company, the shareholders—everybody."

"That's a pretty vivid picture," Tom replied. "Even though we talk about how important development is, I don't think many of us look at it like a lifeline for people."

"And here's one more thing to think about," said David. "A lot of organizations take the position that individual employees are mainly responsible for their own development. The company and the managers are there to support people, but it's up to employees to make sure it happens."

"That's pretty much the way we feel about it here, too," Tom said. "So, don't you agree with that?"

"For the most part, yes—but only up to a point," said David. "Truth is, some people are just naturally better at figuring out how to chart and follow a successful development plan. What's more, some managers are much more skilled than others at helping people sort through the tangle of things they have to consider in making good development choices. And most organizations do a pretty lame job of equipping managers to play that role well."

"Guilty as charged," Tom acknowledged. "We tell managers it's an important part of their responsibility, but I'm sure they're getting mixed signals when we also say that employees are really ultimately responsible for their own development."

"On top of that, no one really holds them accountable for it," David added. "Nobody's really looking closely at how well managers are supporting and encouraging development for the employees who report to them."

"So, I'm guessing all of this might have some implications for the dreaded performance appraisal process," said Tom.

"Good guess."

"Okay, tell me how to make it something that people find meaningful and manageable."

"First of all, you have to stop calling it an 'appraisal' process—for a couple of reasons," said David. "Number one is because adult human beings don't like being judged, especially when they think the judge isn't qualified to pass judgment."

"You have no idea how many times I've heard that," said Tom.

"Sure I do, and here's why," said David. "No matter how hard you try to avoid it, performance appraisals are pretty subjective. Sure, there are some jobs where the objective facts are very clear, and in those cases you don't need a grade because the facts speak for themselves. When a major league hitter has a .350 batting average, you don't need a report card to tell anyone he's a strong performer. But that's not the case with most jobs, and the more white-collar work that people do in an organization, the more subjective the evaluations tend to be."

"We get that from a lot of employees who feel they got a raw deal in a performance review," said Tom. "And they're frustrated that they can't do anything about it because their work isn't very measurable."

"To make it worse, sometimes it's not really a performance issue that gets low ratings for people," said David. "It's because they don't get along with their supervisors, and they get slapped with a notoriously deadly appraisal label, the dreaded *bad attitude*. I'll admit, sometimes people carry a lot of crap with them into the workplace, but sometimes they just aren't naturally open and friendly and enthusiastic. Other people don't like their style or they just don't fit in, and they get labeled as someone who needs an attitude adjustment."

"I know what you mean," said Tom. "Then on the flip side, you've got people who are marginal performers, and they get good ratings because everyone likes them—including their supervisors."

"And it's not because their supervisors are making bad judgments," David added quickly. "They're just people, too, and people are subjective by nature. That's why it's so important to design the evaluation process that eliminates the negative influences of subjective bias as much as possible."

"It's hard, but I do get what you're saying," said Tom. "You said there were two reasons not to call it an appraisal process, though. What's the second one?"

"The second reason is that you want to create positive energy around the process," said David. "So call it performance *development* instead of appraisal."

Tom rolled his eyes.

"I know what you're thinking," David continued, "but don't get me wrong—I hate euphemisms as much as the next guy. You clearly have to change the substance, not just the label, but words do matter, and shifting your language from *appraisal* to *development* makes a difference."

"I guess I can see that," said Tom somewhat reluctantly. "So what about the substance?"

"You have to start by making the process really deliver on what the word *development* implies," David replied. "Let me ask you, Tom, if your goal really is development more than rating and grading people, what would you do differently?"

"Well, we probably wouldn't chalk up all the strengths on one side of the ledger and all of the shortcomings on the other side," said Tom. "You can almost see people cringe when you do that."

"That's what you meant about your own personal reaction to good grades and bad grades," said David.

"Exactly," Tom replied. "After that, it's pretty much what we discussed before: looking at what the employee wants to achieve in his work and in his career, and seeing how those aspirations match up with what we expect the employee to do—and what we think they're capable of doing. I think we do a pretty decent job of that—at least most of our managers do."

"And what if their aspirations don't match your expectations or your assessment of their capabilities?" asked David.

"Then we'd try to find a better match—maybe even a new position for the person," Tom replied. "If they do line up, then we'd put together a learning program and keep track of how they're doing. And to your point earlier, we probably can tell how they're doing without giving them a grade."

"That's great, Tom. But there are a few things you need to do in that process, or it can become just an appraisal in disguise."

"Like what?"

"First, be sure to tie the process to the overall company strategies and priorities," said David. "I don't mean just a summarized list of corporate goals. I mean the real nitty-gritty. People want to know what's behind those goals, why they were chosen, what's happening in the market. They want to know what's going on in the black box of management thinking that leads to their decisions and goals. Too many organizations don't give employees enough credit for being able to understand that level of thinking or to handle it responsibly. They don't really appreciate how employees can help their companies succeed better and how willing they are to deal with tough challenges if they can see how their work connects deep down with the big picture. People really do understand if you do it right … and they really do care."

"I absolutely believe that's true," said Tom.

"Next, you find out how they feel about their work," said David. "I don't mean just whether they feel they did a good job or a bad one, but whether or not their work is enhancing the quality of their lives, going even deeper than the personal aspirations you mentioned. If it's not making their lives better, talk about what that person and the company can do together to improve it. If it is a positive force in their lives, talk about what you can do together to take it to the next level and make it even better."

"I can see how that would make the process a lot more meaningful for everyone—and certainly more agreeable than a typical appraisal session," said Tom. "It also would be more productive."

"That's the first step," said David. "Then you review people's progress on their learning plan at least twice a year, not annually. Even if the person needs longer-term development, make sure you have major milestones at six-month intervals to check up on them along the way."

"That makes a lot of sense to me," said Tom. "I've always thought that a year was too long to go between performance reviews."

"Finally—and this is where I get a lot of push back from managers— if you want to make the process something that people feel good about, don't drag in all the negative baggage about past performance problems," said David. "You want to acknowledge their successes and contributions, and then build on those strengths. It will make people feel energized and optimistic, and it will give them the fuel for future success."

"So are you saying you can't even breathe a word about people's weak areas?" asked Tom. "When you're talking about improvement, sometimes it's going to stem from areas where people are coming up short, isn't it?"

"Sure, you can look at where people need to improve," said David. "You have to do that. This isn't about acting like Pollyanna. But you can talk about it in terms of what the improvement is going to allow the person to do and how it's going to help people aspire to their personal and professional ambitions."

"Okay, that sounds very sweet," said Tom with a touch of sarcasm. "But what are you supposed to do about genuine performance problems? Put on a smiley face and pretend that everything is rosy and nice?"

"It all depends on your goal," said David. "Is it about getting better—or getting even?"

"That's a bit harsh, don't you think? People have to be held accountable for their actions like you said earlier, right?"

"True enough," agreed David. "But it's a matter of style and timing. When do you think is the best time to confront people with a performance problem?"

"When it happens, of course."

"That's right," said David. "And if you do it then, what possible benefit do you gain from bringing it back up again during a performance development session months later when you're supposed to be focusing on the *future*?"

"I can see your point," said Tom. "But what about the times when you do have to confront those performance problems? We've got a number of official procedures for it, but I still think we could handle it better. Got any ideas?"

"First, you need to listen," said David. "It's easy to jump to conclusions, and sometimes things are going on that you can't see on the surface. But regardless of what comes out of that conversation, you need to do what I told you earlier. If someone's performance slips, be sure to approach them as the *source of the solution, not the cause of the problem*. That means you acknowledge that they didn't mess up on purpose, and you show that you trust them to figure out the situation and get performance back on track. They may need some coaching to assess the problem and develop the solution. They also may need some support in implementing it. But either way, the goal is to acknowledge the problem without putting the person on the spot, and give them responsibility for fixing it."

"I have to admit," said Tom, "that approach sounds very appealing— and it's a lot more in tune with what the OD experts are preaching these days. It's not going to be an easy shift for some people, though— especially getting rid of the rating game."

"I think you're going to find that a lot more people will support it than you think," said David. "It's pretty clear that not many people like the typical appraisal process. As for the rating part, here's something a very wise leader of a very successful company told me one time. After years of trying to make their appraisal process truly objective, he gave up and decided to focus on development and leave the appraisals to God because no one else has figured out how to do it right."

Tom realized he had crossed an important threshold. There was only one response he could give.

"Amen," he said.

Focus on development and leave the appraisals to God because no one else has figured out how to do it right.

chapter 7
Sincere Trust and Belief

This was the big day. Tom's interview for the VP job was scheduled for three o'clock. He felt surprisingly calm, considering how anxious he had been feeling just a few days before. Whatever else might have accounted for his confidence, he knew that part of it was coming from his growing clarity and conviction about how to get the best out of people in the workplace.

Still, there was another vital piece that he had to fit into the overall people puzzle. He'd been turning it over in his mind, and he wanted to talk it over with David before he met with the senior staff later for his interview. He'd arrived early, hoping he could catch David before the day got too crazy.

"You look pretty deep in thought."

Tom looked up to see David standing in his doorway, beaming with his usual cheerful smile.

"Good to see you," Tom replied. "I'm getting ready for this afternoon's interview, and I wanted to talk with you about something before I go in there."

"Judging from the look of relief on your face, I'm guessing it must be pretty important," said David.

"Is it that obvious?" asked Tom.

"It just means you care very deeply about what you're doing," said David. "No need to feel embarrassed about it."

"You're right. I can't remember when I've felt so strongly about the work I'm doing—and what it means to our company and the people who work here."

"So what's this hot topic you want to discuss?"

"You remember I told you that I have a thirteen-year-old son?" asked Tom.

"You said you had a teenager, but I didn't know if it was a boy or a girl," David replied.

"Yeah, his name is Michael," said Tom. "We've called him Mikey most of his life. I know it sounds like a little kid's name, but he's always been fine with it—until now."

"Let me guess," said David. "It probably has something to do with sports or girls, right?"

"Not this time," replied Tom with a chuckle. "You see, last Saturday night, Mikey wanted to go hang out at the mall with his friends. He's asked us before, and my wife and I just don't like the whole idea. We've seen too many kids hanging around in malls, and they weren't behaving the way I'd like my son to behave in public. We're also concerned for his safety."

"So you said no, and the typical parent-teenager battle ensued, right?" asked David.

"You guessed it," replied Tom. "He wanted to know why he couldn't go, peppering us with all kinds of questions—if we thought he didn't know how to behave, if we felt he was irresponsible, if we didn't believe in him, and on and on. Then he hit us with the same question he always asks when we don't give in: Why don't you trust me?"

"Ouch," replied David. "I'm sure that had to sting."

"Yeah, and I gave pretty much the same answer I usually give him. It sounded decent then, but it seems a bit lame now that I think about it," said Tom. "I told him, 'It's not that I don't trust you, Mikey—it's just that I know how boys your age can be when they get in group like that, and I'm afraid you might run into some trouble you can't handle.' Something like that."

"To which he replied?" asked David.

"He said it still sounded like we didn't trust him," Tom replied. "And then he laid another big one on us … a new one this time."

"What's that?" asked David.

"He said he was tired of being treated like a kid," Tom answered. "And then he said, 'By the way, I don't want you to call me Mikey anymore. My friends call me Mike, and that's the way I like it.' Then he went to his room and closed the door. It's the first time I ever felt like I'd really lost touch with him."

"I'm sure you realize you didn't lose touch," said David. "You just lost some of the control that you've been used to having over your children. That can be pretty unsettling for a parent."

"You're right," Tom acknowledged. "We've been pretty protective of our kids, and we know eventually we have to let them step out so they can take some control over their own lives. But it's hard."

"So, is that what you wanted to talk about before your meeting?" asked David.

"Sort of," Tom replied. "Do you remember when we talked about the need for employees to have the right balance between freedom and control?"

"Of course," David replied with a nod.

"Well, I hate to say it, but it's like the situation with Mikey—I mean, Mike," Tom admitted. "When it comes to our employees, I think we're on the side of control because we don't trust them enough. Then we wind up treating them as though they're kids, just like you said a few days ago."

"And then they go to their rooms and shut the door," said David with a knowing smile. "Not literally, of course—unless they work in an office that actually *has* a door. Instead, they just turn away and shut themselves down from giving you anything but what you absolutely demand of them."

"Exactly," said Tom. "So here's my question: How can you convince people you really trust them without turning over the keys to the castle? I know you said that employees don't expect to have total freedom to do whatever they want on the job. But it always feels like people are saying 'You don't trust me' whenever a manager questions them about something or says no to something they want to do."

"First of all, listen to the language you're using," replied David. "Have you heard the old saying 'A man convinced against his will is of the same opinion still'? So, you have a choice. You can either wear yourself out trying to *convince* people that you trust them—or you can just trust them. If you do that, they don't need any convincing."

"Okay, Mr. Distinctions," Tom replied a bit sarcastically. "Explain the difference."

"Do you remember when I told you what *won't* work if you're trying to get people on board with a new employee improvement program?" asked David.

"Quite a few things, as I recall," Tom replied. "One in particular is that words matter, but actions matter most."

"Bingo! And the same thing is true for trust," said David. "Go back to the improvement process. If you set it up in a way that genuinely encourages employee initiative, if you approve their ideas on the spot, and if you actively support them in implementing the improvements, then you don't need any words. You don't need any convincing."

"Okay, so what else did I say wrong?" asked Tom.

"Well, you slipped back into the old pattern of sounding like employees are supposed to be good little soldiers and just follow their managers' orders when they tell them what to do," replied David.

"I can see what you mean," said Tom. "It's so easy to fall into the kind of language that makes it sound like we're dealing with kids instead of working with responsible adults."

"It doesn't work very well with kids either, but let's stick with people in the workplace for right now," David replied. "I know you're familiar with the term *servant leader*. Unfortunately, it's gotten so misused that people are getting jaundiced and misguided about it. But it's an important concept. A vital part of a manager's role clearly is to serve and support people. In fact, it's much more crucial than giving orders and telling employees what they can and can't do. Let's face it, most employees already know those things pretty well."

"So, let me give it another try," Tom requested. "What do we need to do to demonstrate that we sincerely trust and believe in the people who work here?"

"That sounds pretty great," David replied. "Before we tackle that one, though, let's look at it from the flip side. What does *management* have to do in order for *employees* to trust *them*?"

"Okay," Tom agreed. "But it seems like the two things go hand in hand, don't they?"

"You bet they do," David replied. "Trust is definitely a two-way street. But here's the tricky part. Even though they go hand in hand, that doesn't mean that both sides bear equal responsibility for making it work."

"I don't understand."

"Building trust always has to start with management because they're holding most of the cards," said David. "They're the ones dictating direction and calling the shots. They're the ones in control—and they're the ones who decide how much of that control they're willing to share."

"So, are you saying that managers are responsible for trusting employees *and* for getting employees to trust us?" asked Tom skeptically.

"I can tell you don't like the sound of that idea very much," David replied.

"You have to admit, it sounds pretty one-sided," Tom said. "Help me understand this 'two-way street' that sounds like it's really only going one way."

"It's kind of like your situation with Mike. He really hasn't done anything to make you *not* trust him, right?" David asked as Tom nodded in reply. "And even if you tell him your decision is not a matter of trust, that's how it looks to him. Since you're the one in control of the ultimate decision about whether or not he goes to the mall, he also feels like his opinion doesn't mean anything. To make matters worse, there's nothing he can do about it. So his self-esteem is in the tank because he feels you don't trust him, and on top of that he feels powerless because he still can't do what he wants. Starting to catch my drift here?"

"I can see one thing for sure," Tom replied. "Not feeling trusted is tough enough when you're a kid. It has to be frustrating as hell for adults in the workplace who want more control over decisions that affect their jobs and their lives."

"Especially when a lot of the time they really *do* know what direction to take better than their 'parents' on the job do," added David.

"Okay, so, tell me what we have to do to get employees to trust management," asked Tom. "What does that take?"

"You start with the two main needs that I said drive people's feelings and behaviors," David replied. "Remember what they are?"

"You mean security and self-esteem?" asked Tom.

"That's right," David replied. "Like I said before, when those two needs are met, people perform well. When they aren't met, they perform poorly. They're the bedrock of human behavior. If you ever wonder why people aren't lining up for what you're dishing out to them, that's the first place to look."

"It sounded pretty simplistic the first time you said it, but I'm getting a deeper appreciation for how important it is," Tom answered. "Okay, what's next after self-esteem and security?"

"I know how much you like my lists, so here's another one for you," David replied as he reached into his pocket and handed Tom a sheet of paper.

Tom smiled as he took the list and read it.

Building employee trust in management:

- Caring

- Honesty and openness

- Responsiveness

- Competence

- Reliability

- Apology and accountability

"I'm not even going to ask how you already knew I'd want to talk with you about trust," said Tom as he looked at the list. "I know these things are important, David, but they look pretty basic to me—sort of like motherhood and apple pie."

"You're absolutely right," said David. "There's nothing mysterious about this list—or any of the lists I've shown you. They pretty much speak for themselves. What matters most is your *perspective* on them. The challenge is not to delude yourself into thinking that management is actually demonstrating these attributes when employees see the situation very differently."

"True enough," Tom agreed.

"Take *caring*, for example," said David. "If the company is going to get rid of a hundred people, is it enough to give those employees two weeks' notice and two weeks of severance pay—along with the obligatory tribute from the CEO written by someone else, telling them how much the company appreciates their many years of dedicated service? Or are you going to provide a comprehensive plan for helping them make the transition to another job, or maybe even another career? Have you given them the training to increase their chances for a better job than the one they were hired for? Are you going to put a systematic process in place for supporting the 'survivors' who are losing close friends and wondering how they're going to manage the workload with a hundred fewer people?"

"I know what you mean," said Tom. "We've tried to take factors like that into consideration in the past, and I think we've improved how we handle those situations a lot—but it's a big undertaking."

"That's why most companies just decide to do it fast—make a clean break, as they like to say," David replied. "They try to push the remaining people into new routines as quickly as possible. They tell them how important it is stay focused, and they give them the old bromide about how they want everyone to work smarter, not harder. No time for grief. No time for reflection. No effort to confer with the remaining people on how their departments can operate most effectively going forward. There's nothing very clean about that kind of approach from an employee's point of view."

"Like I said, it's tricky," Tom replied. "Sometimes it's tough to do everything you'd like to do, especially when there are lots of people involved. But we try to do the best we can."

"I'm not trying to be judgmental," said David. "I'm sure you're doing some good things for people. All I'm saying is this: there's an old saying that goes 'people don't care how much you know until they know how much you care.' To the extent that employees feel you're falling short in the way you care for their well-being, their level of trust will be diminished. It's not a yes-or-no issue. It's a matter of degrees."

"So, what else can you tell me about gaining trust?

"The sequence of the qualities on that list is important, too," David replied. "If people don't believe that you genuinely care about them, being honest isn't going to win you many points. And even if you care and you're honest, they're not going to trust you, if you're not responsive. And even if you're responsive, you're on shaky ground if they think you're incompetent. And even if people think you know what you're doing, you won't gain their trust if they don't think they can count on you to follow through on your promises. And even if you do all of that, you're still going to screw up sometimes, and when you do, you need to own up to the mistake, say you're sorry and tell folks how you're going to fix things. See what I mean?"

"Yes, I do—and it makes a lot of sense," Tom agreed. "So, let's come back to the flip side of the coin. How can we demonstrate that we sincerely trust and believe in the people who work here?"

"Sure," David replied. "It's actually a pretty short trip from the conversation we've been having already. I told you a few minutes ago that it's futile to try and convince people that you trust them." Tom nodded as David continued. "What's more, you really don't need to work at convincing anyone as long as you do the things that *demonstrate* that you trust them."

"Such as?" Tom asked.

"Okay, let's take honesty and openness," David replied. "When you explain the details of a dicey situation to employees in a way that's authentic and candid, you're demonstrating that you trust their ability to handle the information like responsible adults. They appreciate that kind of openness, and they know the difference between communicating like that and being spoon-fed morsels of informational mush like they're infants. It's the whole kid thing again."

"Yeah, that's pretty clear," said Tom. "So what do you have to do next?"

"Well, then you have to watch out for the *program trap*," said David.

"Sounds like that has something to do with the difference you pointed out earlier between a program and process, right?" asked Tom.

"Absolutely," David said. "I can't emphasize enough how critical that distinction is if you want to show people that you mean what you say. Programs are easy to spot because there's a lot of flag waving and promotional hype with few if any imbedded systems and processes to support them. You also get only some of the people participating, and those who are doing it only do it once in a while. On top of that, programs usually look pretty phony to employees."

"Can you give me an example?" Tom asked.

"I've got a great one, actually," David replied. "No too long ago, I was working with a group of employees at a company that was trying to get people on board with their new quality initiative. Someone had just draped a banner across the front of the building that said, 'Quality is our pride and commitment'—a sure indicator of the program trap. I asked the employees what they thought of it, and one seasoned veteran summed it up for everyone."

"I'll bet he didn't get up and wave any pom-poms," Tom remarked.

"How'd you guess?" David asked wryly. "He said, 'You know, I've been at this company for twenty-five years, and there are only two signs that mean anything around here. One is "Exit," and the other is "Wet Paint." Everything else is just plain bullshit.' All the employees in the room laughed and applauded."

"I guess that pretty well says it all," Tom said. "What did you do?"

"Well, I didn't join in with the applause," David replied. "But I couldn't hold back the laughter. It was just too classic, and the way the guy delivered it was so darned funny."

"Yeah, and if there's one thing I've learned about group dynamics in most companies, longtime employees like that often have a lot of influence on the opinions of their coworkers," Tom added.

"You bet they do," David agreed. "Sometimes even more than managers do, especially if the person also happens to be a strong performer that employees like and respect. But if you can avoid the artificial nonsense of the program trap—and implement a true *process* that everyone is responsible for and everyone is held accountable for—people will be more inclined to take you seriously."

"And when that process gives employees the freedom to make improvements on their own initiative day after day, they know you mean it when you say you trust them," Tom added.

"You got it," David acknowledged. "And that goes for every process that has anything to do with employee relations. It's about your processes for measuring performance: rewards and recognition, communication, learning and development, continuous improvement, and everything else. If those processes don't support your claims that you trust people, that you truly believe people are your most important asset—well, then you're wasting your breath."

"We've talked about most of those things," said Tom, "but I want to get more of your thoughts on communication. Every time we do an employee survey, that's one of the top two or three things that we get dinged on. I'd sure love to figure out how we can crack the code on that one."

"You better be careful," said David with a smile. "You push the communication button with me, and I could go on for days."

"I hope you can give me an abbreviated version," Tom pleaded playfully. "My interview with the senior staff is this afternoon, remember?"

As if on cue, Tom's cell phone rang. "Wonder who that is," Tom said as he reached into his pocket. Looking at the display, he could see that it was someone from his department.

"Hey, Joan, what are you doing in so early?" Tom asked.

Tom smiled as he listened to the reply. "Okay, hotshot, I'll be there in a few minutes."

"I've got to look at something right away," said Tom as he put the phone back in his pocket. "Our benefits manager has been working on a new medical plan, and it's been quite a challenge for her. You know what it's like these days trying to keep healthcare costs under control and still keep employees happy with the coverage."

David nodded as Tom continued.

"Well, Joan is very excited because she thinks she's come up with something that could be an important breakthrough, and she wants to get my reaction to it right away. Could we pick up the conversation about communication in a little bit?"

"I like your priorities," David replied with a smile of approval. "You're on the brink of a pretty big breakthrough of your own. It's nice to see you appreciate how that feels to someone else, too."

"I'm beginning to appreciate a lot of things more than ever before," said Tom.

"Oh, I doubt it," David said gently. "I suspect your capacity for appreciation is about the same as it's always been. It's your sense of hope that's gotten a big boost."

Tom acknowledged David with a nod and a smile. "So, will you be here in an hour or so?"

"You can count on it," David said.

As David got up to walk out the door, Tom's expression made it clear that he was still wondering what David was really doing at the company.

"You're working way too hard to figure me out," David said before Tom had a chance to say what was on his mind. "Just go talk with Joan, and …" David paused momentarily with a teasing grin for dramatic effect. "And when you're done, come down to my office for some insights on *real* communication."

The only way to make a man trustworthy is to trust him. (Henry Stimson)

chapter 8
Real-Life, Real-Time Communication

Tom was short of breath as he rushed into David's office.

"Oh, I'm glad you're still here," Tom said. "It took longer than I expected."

"Breakthroughs usually do," replied David. "So what did you think of Joan's idea?"

"It's hard to tell yet," Tom answered. "It's pretty complicated, and we have to run some numbers to see how it would play out. But she's definitely brought some fresh thinking to the whole thing, and it's great to see how pumped up she's feeling about it."

"So how do you think she would rate the quality of communication right now if she were filling out one of your employee surveys?" David asked.

Tom thought for a moment before he answered the question. "I'm not sure," he replied. "I guess I never really thought of that kind of conversation as something employees consider when they rate us on communication."

"So when you get low ratings, what do you think they're complaining about?" David asked.

"I've always assumed that they're mainly telling us we're not giving them enough information, and that what we do give them isn't timely enough," Tom replied.

"That's part of it," said David. "And if you're like most companies, one way you respond to those surveys is to create new methods for distributing information and sending out messages."

"Yeah, that's one thing we do," Tom said. "Judging from your tone, though, that's not exactly what you'd recommend."

"Believe me, Tom," replied David, "when people complain about poor communications, they're usually not telling you they want *more* publications or *more* employee meetings or *more* management messages streaming through your intranet."

"I have to admit those tactics haven't done much to improve our survey scores on communication," Tom confessed.

"You're not alone," said David. "That's why a lot of companies wind up throwing in the towel when it comes to surveys. They come to the conclusion that they're doing enough communicating the way it is, and no matter how much they do, people are always going to complain about it. So they keep doing things basically the same way, making a few tweaks here and there, and they just learn to live with the fallout."

"Well, we haven't gotten to the point where we're ready to just live with it quite yet," said Tom. "But I can't say we're doing enough to fix it either. I'll just bet you've got some ideas on how to deal with it," Tom added with a smile. "Maybe even another list?"

"Amazing how you figured that out," David said as he reached for a paper on the top of his desk.

"Yeah, amazing," Tom replied with a grin.

Real-Life, Real-Time Communication

- Interaction

- Availability of information

- Access to information

- Speed

- Relevance

- Inclusion

"Nice list," Tom smiled appreciatively. "Especially the first thing—interaction. That's really one of my hot buttons. I'm always telling people that we need to do a better job of two-way communication around here."

"Is there any other kind?" David asked pointedly.

"You must be kidding," Tom replied. "We're constantly sending out messages and announcements and making presentations to people without getting any feedback. What's more, we don't really give employees much of a chance to initiate communication upward. It's all pretty much a one-way flow."

"What makes you think that's communication?" asked David.

"I think I hear another distinction coming on," Tom replied.

"Yep, and it's really important to get your head around it," said David. "The point is, communication requires some kind of exchange. One-way communication is like one-handed clapping—pointless. If the information is just going one way, all you've got is message distribution. It's not communication until you get some kind of response. Without any feedback, it's hard to know how people feel about it, if they understand it, what they're going to do with it—or even if they saw it."

"I get the point," Tom acknowledged. "But whatever you call it, a lot of people around here think that all they should have to do is send out a message, and then get the response they expect."

"Okay, well, the next time you hear people complain because they *didn't* get what they wanted when they sent out a message, pretend you're me and ask them a bunch of annoying questions," said David with a smile.

"That sounds like fun. Can you give me some pointers?"

"My pleasure," David replied. "You can start by asking them why they didn't communicate. When they ask you what you mean, or if they get aggravated and declare that they did, ask them how they know. Then when they say they sent out a message to everyone, ask them how they know the message got through and people understood it. Then when they say they shouldn't have to worry about that because people are responsible for reading what people send to them, ask them if they're more interested in being right or getting results—"

"I'm not sure I like where this is heading," Tom interrupted.

"Wait till you hear what's next," David replied. "At this point, if they haven't kicked you out of their office, tell them you sympathize with their problems, but if there isn't a way to close the loop, *it's not communication*. Then tell them that if they're not getting the response they expect, they have no one to blame but themselves."

"Oh, that'll certainly make me popular."

"And while you've got them good and upset, here's a way to aggravate them even more," said David. "Anytime you hear them say they're going to communicate a message *to* someone, tell them they can't. When they screw up their faces like they don't understand, explain that if they really want to communicate, they can only do it *with* someone."

"I can see their reactions now," said Tom. "After a while, people will be so self-conscious about what they say around me, they'll never communicate *to* me or *with* me ever again."

Both men laughed as Tom looked at the other items on the list.

"Availability and access," Tom said. "Why do you have those listed as two different points? Aren't they the same thing?"

"Not really," David replied. "Availability is a matter of *policy*, and if you want to foster trust in your policies, the key is *no secrets*. Access, though, is a matter of *process*, and if you want to foster employee trust in your processes, the key is *no barriers*."

"Tell me more," said Tom.

"Sure," David continued. "You see, an organization may have a policy that all information is open and available. But that doesn't do much good if people can't get access to it. If it's buried somewhere that's impossible to reach, or if they can't process it because they can't understand it, or if they're drowning from information overload, it's pretty useless."

"I can relate to that," said Tom. "We really have tried to be more open with people about information, but they still complain that trying to sort out what's really relevant is like trying to find a needle in haystack sometimes. So how do you balance those two things?"

"There's no single answer," David replied, "but part of dealing with it is the next thing on the list—speed."

"How are those things connected?"

"We've all heard the old saying 'Time is money,' right?" David asked. "Well, here's a newsflash for you. It's true—and speed counts big time when it comes to a company's communication system. The best time for information exchange is *real time*, not weeks, days, or even hours later. As soon as information is in a form that's credible and able to be processed, it should be available and accessible to people."

"But how do you reconcile that idea with complaints about information overload?" asked Tom.

"Remember, I said all relevant information should be available and accessible—not *distributed*," David clarified. "The key is to let people know where it is and how to get it. And even if you have to send something out right away, that doesn't mean you have to share all information with everyone all at once. That's just dumping, not communication."

"That's really tricky in an organization with as many people and locations as ours—and with all the information and knowledge we have to share," Tom said.

"I know what you mean," said David. "Organizations have been struggling with the speed challenge forever. But it's crucial, and the larger you are, the more important it is to do it well. Everyone knows that, but they've been strangled by their own ponderous policies and systems. One of the biggest problems is that they're afraid to communicate with people until the message gets properly packaged in corporate-speak. Do you want to know how employees feel about it? They're saying, 'Get me the real honest-to-goodness information *now*—without sanitizing or glamorizing it. Then we'll trust you, and we can really get something done together.'"

"I'm guessing that's probably why relevance is the next thing on your list," Tom said. "By the time we get done polishing and packaging the information, we've not only lost speed, but employees also wonder just how real and meaningful it is."

"Good guess," David acknowledged. "And there's another important factor about relevance that you talked about a minute ago. Sometimes management overreacts to employee criticism about communication, and they start flooding people with stuff they don't really need or care about. The information misses the mark because it doesn't have much bearing on the day-to-day work lives of most employees. It just doesn't seem very real to them. So they start ignoring messages and hitting the delete button as soon as they pop up in their inboxes."

"So, how do you know where to draw the line?" asked Tom. "How do you strike the right balance between not too much and not enough?"

"It's not just a question of volume," David cautioned. "Once again, it's a matter of relevance. Three sentences can be too much if it doesn't really matter to people. Three paragraphs may not be enough if it's something that's meaningful to them."

"But what's truly relevant to most people?"

"Remember when we talked about measurement?" David asked. "Measurements drive people's behavior—as long as the numbers are meaningful, of course. Share information about significant metrics, and people will pay attention. That's especially true if the numbers are tied to goals and objectives that are important to them—if they have something to do with the real stuff they have to deal with on the job."

"Such as?"

"If you want to know for sure, you have to ask them," David replied. "But some of it's obvious. Take safety, for example. If there's one thing most people care about, it's their personal well-being."

"We do quite a bit around safety at our facilities," said Tom. "We've got safety committees and dedicated safety specialists; we do extensive training for everyone; we've got a lot signage up emphasizing safety and letting people know our safety scores. I think we do pretty well on that one."

"Well, I'll give you a C for 'close, but no cigar,'" David replied.

Tom gave him a surprised look. "Okay, so what's the alternative?"

"Talk about it," David replied quickly. "It's like I was saying earlier. Sending out messages and putting numbers and words on a wall are not the same as communication. And even though it's good to have safety teams, they can get pretty isolated—and you don't see much real dialogue taking place with all the other employees."

"Well, can you give me an example of something we should do?"

"Okay, here's a good one," David offered. "When accidents do happen, get employees together in small groups. Reenact the incident—not literally, of course—but do sort of an instant reply. Figure out how it happened. Talk about how it might happen elsewhere and how it can be prevented from happening again. You can do the same with near misses. That way you get the benefit of learning without anyone getting hurt."

"If we did that with everyone every time we had an incident or a near miss, that would rack up a lot of unproductive hours," Tom said.

"If you've got that many incidents, that's all the more reason to do it—and you don't have do it *every* time," David said. "But think about it, Tom. Think about the kind of signal it would send to employees about the company's commitment to their safety—and how serious you are about making sure people don't get injured. I'll promise you this: if you do something like that, you'll not only have fewer people getting hurt, the time you'll need to spend talking about incidents will go down, too."

"Okay, so what else besides safety can you count on to get people's attention?"

"Just about any number that shows the health of the business," David replied. "If you're paying more than lip service to customer satisfaction, employees will generally tune in to information that will help them boost customer loyalty. They know that happy customers mean better business. And the more actionable that information is, the more relevant it's going to be to people."

"Makes sense," said Tom. "What else?"

"Success stories," said David. "Remember, we already talked about how people love being on a winning team, so they like to hear when the company makes a big score. Basically, Tom, if you want people to pay attention to information and get engaged in the communication process, make sure the information is more operational than promotional. People don't want to be *sold* on what you're doing. They want to be *engaged* in what you're doing, and they need the real story in order to do that."

"That's why we do town hall meetings," said Tom, expecting some sign of approval from David.

"You mean town hall *lectures*, don't you?" David replied to Tom's surprise.

"What do you mean?" Tom shot back defensively.

"Let's be honest, Tom. Most town hall meetings aren't very interactive. You usually get management talking and making presentations the vast majority of the time."

"Sure, we give an update on company performance, and we lay out our performance expectations," said Tom. "But we also give people a chance to ask questions and let us know what's on their minds."

"And I'm sure hundreds of hands shoot up in the air, right?"

"Okay, so not everyone gets directly involved in the discussion," Tom admitted. "Still, they all have a chance to talk if they want to, and even if they don't, they get to hear what other people are thinking and asking. Then everyone gets to hear what management has to say when they respond to the questions."

"I know you have good intentions, Tom," replied David, "but communication is not a spectator sport. If people aren't talking and listening *both* ways, they simply aren't communicating."

"Okay, I get your point," Tom acknowledged. "But even if everyone did want to talk, it would take days for all our employees to ask a question or make a comment. That's just not practical."

"I'll tell you what's not practical," David replied, "and that's expecting employees to feel comfortable standing up in front of hundreds of their coworkers and asking questions or giving their opinions to senior management about things they have on their minds."

"So what should we do?" asked Tom. "Stop doing the quarterly meetings? They may not be perfect, but I know some employees look forward to them, and I think shutting them down would send a bad signal to people."

"I agree," David said. "Look, Tom, there's nothing wrong with all-employee meetings, but if you really want to give people a chance to communicate, make the format more interactive."

"How's that?"

"Think about the meeting you had with Joan a little while ago or your discussion with Mary," David replied. "Can you imagine having that conversation in front of a hundred people? Fact is, people prefer talking in small groups. They feel safer. They feel more comfortable. That's what it takes for people to open up. So, break people into small groups—six to eight in each one. Give them some important questions or issues to discuss. Then have them pick one person from each group to give a brief report to the large group on what each of the smaller groups discussed."

"I like the general idea," Tom said. "But it sounds like that would take a lot more time than we have for the typical town hall meeting."

"Not really," David said. "Even if you have the small groups talk for only about ten to fifteen minutes, you can generate a lot of energy and give just about everyone a chance to talk. Then the person speaking for the group can share the ideas they had in a two-minute report. They can also ask a question if they want. And you don't have to get every group to report. You can do the whole thing in less than an hour. And if they have other questions, you can collect them and respond to them later on your intranet."

"I'm still not sure about the logistics, but it feels right, and I definitely want to talk with some folks about how we might pull it off," said Tom. "Any other ideas about how to build *real* communication into those meetings?"

"Absolutely, and this one doesn't pose the same kind of logistical challenge," David replied. "After the town hall meeting, make it required for all managers to meet for thirty minutes with their teams and talk about what they heard. Discuss what it means for their part of the business. Let people offer suggestions on how to respond. Give them a chance to ask questions in a smaller, less intimidating environment."

"That sounds very doable," said Tom. "Frankly, it's what you'd hope managers are doing anyway, but I think it makes sense to formalize it."

"Here's one more thing you can do to close the communication loop. Everyone's familiar with the term *cascade* when it comes to getting information to flow all the way from top to bottom," David said. Tom nodded. "Well, it's not really a very good metaphor because a cascade only goes one way—top down. Instead, think about communication like a *fountain*: the flow goes up and down and back up again in a continuous cycle. So after the managers have their team meetings, they should send a brief report back up the management chain about the discussions they had. That way, the people who led the town hall meetings can hear the questions and comments that employees had about what was covered at the meeting."

"I like that idea a lot," Tom said. "Not only will our senior folks get more feedback, but it's also likely to be more candid. The whole process really goes right to the heart of the next item on your list—inclusion."

"You're right—and that's just from the town hall meeting," David said. "What's more important is how you communicate with employees—or not—on the job every day. The consequences are a lot more critical than most companies realize. It's really pretty simple. Leaving someone out of the communication loop is like severing the nerves to part of the body—they may still be alive, but they're basically nonfunctional. And the rest of the organization feels the pain, too, one way or another."

"We've tried to work with our managers to get them communicating more effectively with the people who report to them," Tom said. "But we've got a long way to go."

"Part of that challenge for managers goes back to wanting to maintain control or thinking they just don't have enough time," David said. "A lot of managers take the position that employees get the information they *need,* even if it's not always what they *want.*"

"So, what do you say to people like that?" Tom asked.

"I tell them they're partly right," David replied. "Sure, people can get by on a need-to-know basis, but what's the lost opportunity cost? What's more, how much do you think you damage the trust that employees have in their managers when you cut them off from the flow of valuable information?"

"It keeps coming back to trust, doesn't it?" Tom observed thoughtfully. He was silent for a moment and then asked, "Okay, well, what about your last point—authenticity?"

"It's a close cousin of honesty and openness, but it goes a bit deeper," replied David. "Let me ask you something: Have you ever dealt much with antiques?"

"A little," said Tom. "We've got a few at home, but nothing very expensive. Why do you ask?"

"When it comes to antiques, authenticity is crucial," said David. "Have you ever heard antique experts tell people, 'Whatever you do, don't clean up an antique to make it look nice and new and pretty'?"

"Yes, I have," Tom replied. "In fact, that's what an antique dealer told us about an old chest we were going to have refinished. He said it would diminish the value."

"That's because shining it up would reduce its authenticity," said David. "That's the same problem organizations often have with communication. They have a tendency to 'shine it up' instead of being authentic about it. They want to put the right spin on it. If it's good news, they want to glamorize it. If it's bad, they want to sanitize it."

"Been there, done that," said Tom, as though making a confession.

"To carry the analogy with antique furniture a bit further, that's what people mean when they say they want the 'unvarnished truth,'" said David. "Can you see how it diminishes trust when communication gets too slick and thick?"

"Absolutely," Tom replied. "In fact, I can see how everything you're saying about *real* communication makes your point that management needs to be responsible for both sides of the two-way street of trust. If we're open and inclusive and straight with people—if we show them we trust their ability to handle delicate or difficult information—they're more likely to respond in kind."

"That's right," said David. "But I don't want to make it sound simplistic. Management can be messy business at times, and lots of unpleasant things can cause people to give less than their best—fear, resentment, anger, revenge, confusion, you name it. Any of them can undermine trust. But if you've got a solid foundation of communication principles and practices, at least you stand a better chance of recovering when things do get rocky."

"You know, David, I was just thinking that a lot of this stuff comes down to living by the Golden Rule."

"The Golden Rule is wonderful," David replied. "In fact, virtually every religion in the world has some form of that principle as a tenet of their faith. Aside from religion, it's just part of what it takes for human beings to get along with one another."

"Yeah, so it sounds like there's another point you're trying to make."

"That rule is also the bedrock of security and self-esteem," David continued. "But some people—some managers, especially—really do believe in being pretty tough in the workplace. They've come up through the old school—that's how they made it through the ranks, and they're not about to give it up now that they're in the driver's seat."

"Is that because they don't believe in the Golden Rule, or do they really think that being tough is the best way to manage?" asked Tom.

"It's not about wanting to be tough on people, and most folks understand that you get what you give in life for the most part," said David. "It's just that control thing again. They feel responsible, and they don't want to take a chance of something going wrong by letting people go off and do things on their own initiative."

Tom paused for a moment, reflecting on the things that he and David had been discussing.

"You know, David, it's getting tougher all the time to do a good job of managing communication with employees. Their expectations are changing, and we know we need to share more information. We also need to do it faster, just like you said, but how do you keep up with it all?"

"Just remember one very important lesson," David replied. "Instead of trying to be a great communicator, focus on being a great *communication facilitator*."

"What do you mean?"

"What would you say if I told you that communication is too important to be left in the hands of professional communicators?"

"I'd say you're trying to mess with my head again," Tom replied with a smile. "But I know you're trying to make a point."

"Sometimes, it's the only way I can get communications people to grasp a basic reality," David said. "Truth is, most of the communication that takes place in an organization has very little to do with the messages communicators craft and the media they manage. So if the organization is going to improve its communication as a whole, professional communicators like you need to concentrate on helping everyone else take responsibility for it. And you need to help them learn how to do it well."

"I know that's true, and we've got to do it," Tom acknowledged. "It's just hard to let go of the controls—and it'll be tough to get everyone's communication skills and knowledge where they need to be."

"Not nearly as tough as trying to keep doing it all yourself."

Tom paused momentarily, looking at David. "In case you haven't noticed, I've been getting a lot of help the past few days. Any chance I count on getting more?"

"I have a feeling you've gotten about all the help you're going to need from me," David replied. "I think you're ready to handle it on your own from here. In fact, you've been ready all along."

"I don't understand," said Tom, feeling as though something important was about to slip away.

"You will," David replied. "Soon … very soon."

One-way communication is like one-handed clapping – it's pointless.

chapter 9

Imagine That

I t was time. As Tom got on the elevator and headed for the boardroom, he knew his life would never be the same. Regardless of what came out of the interview, he felt he was ready to go places that he had only imagined just a few short days before.

When he stepped out of the elevator at the top floor, he felt a strange sensation as he walked down the hall. For some odd reason, all the offices were empty. None of the executive assistants were at their desks. The whole place had an eerie calm about it.

As he walked along, he felt a breeze coming toward him. Ahead at the end of the hall, he could see windows open and curtains waving back and forth. *That's odd, he thought to himself. I've never seen windows in the boardroom before.*

But the thought passed quickly. Tom's attention was focused on seizing the moment and making the most of the opportunity he was getting to help reshape the future of the company.

Stepping into the room, he stopped dead in his tracks as he glanced at the head of the table. Seated in the CEO's chair was … David, smiling and not saying a word. Then Tom began to notice others in the room. Mary, the receptionist, was sitting at David's right. Tom's son, Mike, was next to her. And sitting to David's left was none other than Barney the purple dinosaur.

"Come on in and have a seat," said David. "We've all been looking forward to meeting with you."

Tom wasn't sure what to do. His thoughts were jumbled, and he was afraid to say something that might tip them off to his bewilderment. Was the management team testing him somehow? Was David part of a grand scheme to see if was ready for the VP position? And what the heck was Mike doing here? He was supposed to be at school! And what about Barney? If this was some kind of practical joke, he decided he'd better play along.

"So, it looks like the management team decided to bring in some real experts for this interview," Tom said, smiling and trying to sound unsurprised. "Couldn't handle it on their own, I guess, huh?"

"We thought it would be nice for you to have a few close friends with you," David replied. "We wanted to give you a little moral support."

"I appreciate that," Tom said without skipping a beat. "So when is the management team going to show up?"

"Oh, they're right outside," David replied, pointing toward the open window. "They're waiting for you to join them."

"Outside? What do you mean?" asked Tom with stunned surprise. "We're twenty floors high."

"Take a look," said David. "Barney's been giving them flying lessons."

Tom's face turned pale. His confusion turned to anxiety as he walked slowly toward the window.

"Go ahead," said David. "Take a leap."

"What?" Tom gasped.

"You can do it," David replied calmly as he and the others got up from their seats and started walking slowly toward Tom. "You've been ready for a long time, and we're all here to help you take your next step. And if you need a flying lesson, Barney is set to help you out."

"You know, David," Tom said backing away from the window with a forced calmness in his voice. "I'm beginning to think I may not be ready for this position. I've always been a bit afraid of heights," he added, trying to escape with a touch of humor.

"Of course you're ready," said David, pointing toward the window. "You're just as good as those guys out there."

Tom glanced outside, amazed to see the management team flying around calmly in the clear blue sky. He was sweating now. His heart was pounding as he inched by toward the door, determined to make a run for it.

But where the door had been a moment ago there was a whiteboard and sheets of paper floating in midair with David's lists scrawled on them. Suddenly, the lists faded away, and in their place in bold, blazing letters were these words: "Imagination without free will has no power. Free will without imagination has no purpose."

He turned back to run, only to have Barney grasp him with his big purple arms, lifting him in the air and pulling him toward the open window. As Tom struggled to break free, he fell to the floor, pulling Barney down on top of him.

"Okay, people," Tom hollered as he attempted to push Barney away. "This whole thing has gone far enough. Get off me!" He continued to struggle, growing more and more frantic. "Let me go!"

Then he heard a familiar voice from the other side of the room, saying, "Tom, what on earth are you doing?"

He recognized the voice, but he couldn't see anyone.

"Tom," came the voice again. "Wake up."

Suddenly everything went dark as Tom finally managed to push Barney off him. As he broke free, he heard a crashing noise and thought, with horror, that he must have pushed Barney through a windowpane. Then the familiar voice spoke once again.

"Honey, are you all right?"

Tom bolted upright and looked around, completely bewildered.

"That must've been quite a dream," the voice said.

Tom shook his head and looked at his wife, who was sitting next to him holding his arm. He stared at her in disbelief for what seemed to be several minutes.

Then he broke the silence. "A dream?" Slowly the fog began to clear. "I can't believe it, Jennifer. It seemed so real. I mean, you wouldn't believe everything that happened."

"Well, whatever it was, I hope it was worth the cost of a new lamp," Jennifer said with a smile as she pointed to the other side of the room. There lay his pillow alongside fragments of glass strewn across the bedroom floor.

"Oh, honey, I'm sorry," said Tom as he got up to clean up the mess.

"I'll take care of it," said Jennifer. "You grab another pillow from the closet. Care to tell me what the dream was about?"

"I don't know where to start," Tom replied. "It was mainly about all the stuff going on at work. I'm sure my conversation with Marie last night is what triggered the whole thing … but it got really weird."

"What do you mean?" asked Jennifer.

"There was this guy named David who was a consultant and was talking with me about all kinds of things. Mikey was in it, too. And you'll never believe this … so was Barney."

"Barney who?" asked Jennifer.

"Barney the dinosaur," Tom replied with a grin.

"So, let me guess—that's the part of your dream that was weird, right?" asked Jennifer teasingly.

"Yeah, and that's just for starters—a classic case of an overactive imagination."

"Well, you know what you always tell the kids," said Jennifer. "The things you imagine are just as real as the shoes on your feet."

"If I ever had any doubts about that before, I sure don't anymore," Tom said. "But the whole imagination thing is really quite remarkable and mysterious when you think about it."

"I guess I don't see what's so mysterious about it," said Jennifer. "That's just the way people are. It's human nature."

"I've certainly heard *that* comment a lot in the past few days—or the past few hours, I guess," said Tom.

"You need to get some sleep," Jennifer said, smiling and shaking her head. "It's okay to have your head in the clouds as long as you keep your feet on the ground."

"That's a great phrase," Tom said admiringly. "Where did you come up with that one?"

"I don't know. I heard it somewhere a long time ago," she replied. "And anyway, do you think you're the only one with an imagination around here?" asked Jennifer with a smile as she reached over to turn out the light on her nightstand.

"That's not what I meant," said Tom apologetically, continuing to talk in the darkness. "I guess I'm just amazed right now at how people come up with that kind of stuff."

"Well, if a full-grown man can have dreams about Barney the purple dinosaur, I'd say just about anything is imaginable," Jennifer said teasingly.

"Is that any way to talk to the future VP of HR?" asked Tom.

"Go to sleep, Tom," said Jennifer quietly as she drifted off. "Remember … feet on the ground."

"Uh-huh," said Tom as he closed his eyes. "And head in the clouds."

The things you imagine are as real as the shoes on your feet.

chapter 10
The Perfect Fit

Tom wasn't nervous. In fact, he felt pretty good. The interview with senior management had gone well, and the decision was out of his hands. It had been several weeks since Marie had left, and even though he missed her, he was surprised at how free and relaxed he felt. He was also energized and ready to handle whatever came next.

As he waited in the CEO's office, he looked around the room. He'd been there lots of times before, but he'd never paid much attention to the décor, to the feel of the place. Now as he sat there waiting to meet with the man who would decide his fate, he was struck by the simplicity of the furniture and decorations. Aside from a large landscape painting above the sofa, nothing else hung on the walls. The rest of the room was just as spare. No statues. No knickknacks. No papers. Everything was clean and simple.

Only two things offered a glimpse into the man's personal style: several photos of his family scattered about and an exquisitely crafted corner bookshelf filled with an unusual array of books. Some of the books, as Tom expected, were about business. Others were on topics ranging from engineering to philosophy, spirituality, psychology, and more.

The only thing on the desk was a block of wood with the CEO's name, Dan Jenkins, chiseled into it. Judging from the crudeness of the carving, Tom guessed that one of Dan's children or grandchildren had made it for him. He reached over to pick it up so he could examine it more closely. Just then, he heard the door open behind him.

"Pretty nice piece of work, don't you think?" asked Dan with a bit of a chuckle.

Caught off guard, Tom wheeled around to greet the man who was walking into the room. He recovered quickly and replied, "If you're looking for an educated opinion, you're talking to the wrong guy. Compared to the things I've tried to make, anything would look like a masterpiece."

"My older brother made that when we were both in high school," Dan said. "He was good at just about everything. Captain of the football team. Straight-A student. You know the type. And, of course, all the girls swooned over him. We had a great relationship, considering we were only a year apart. I really admired the guy. Still do. I was always trying to live up to the standards he set, but I usually fell a bit short—except for one thing."

"Let me guess," said Tom. "Except for woodworking, right?"

"Back in those days, most of the guys took woodshop," Dan replied. "So, he did his little brother a favor and carved my name into a piece of wood. I really loved it. Then the following year, it was my turn, and I'll never forget the day I brought home the carving I did of his name. The moment I handed his carving to him was the first time I ever saw him look at his little brother with genuine admiration."

"I can imagine how you must've felt," Tom said.

"It was pretty great," said Dan. "Speaking of imagination, that was quite a performance you put on in there today. It's a bit unusual for someone interviewing for an executive position to talk so fervently about Barney the dinosaur."

"Yeah, I'm sure that must've seemed a bit strange," Tom acknowledged.

"I actually thought it was fun—and insightful," Dan said. "So were a lot of other things you said. I don't recall ever hearing you talk like that before."

"Like I told you and the rest of the senior team, I've been doing a lot of thinking about this whole thing, especially since Marie left. I admired her a lot—and still do. She was a super mentor, and I was more than happy to have her lead the way. But when she told me she was leaving, I felt a shift inside of me. I felt this pull to let go and leap into a whole new level of thinking, know what I mean?"

"Absolutely," Dan acknowledged.

"Anyway, as I started working on it, new ideas started taking shape," said Tom. "Actually, that's not quite right. Most of the ideas weren't really all that new. They just started coming together in new ways, and it reshaped the way I saw things."

"Well, you definitely raised some eyebrows with the management team," said Dan.

"I hope that's a good thing," Tom replied. "I know some of what I was saying must've seemed over the top, but I wasn't doing it for novelty or shock value. I was sincere, and I'm convinced it's all relevant to what we need to do here."

"You know, Tom, some of the things you said reminded me of my father," said Dan. "He grew up on a farm in Iowa during the Depression. They barely managed to get by when he was a kid, like most farmers back then. Still, he had a great sense of humor about it. He used to joke that they didn't have enough money to buy birdseed for a cuckoo clock."

Both men laughed as Dan continued.

"He also loved to tell stories about little moments of happiness that they shared in spite of how tough things were. He must've told the story a hundred times about my grandfather walking down the dirt road to their farmhouse one day with a big smile on his face. Somehow he had managed to scrape together a few pennies for some store-bought candy. All five kids were out in the yard, and you would've thought it was Christmas the way they jumped around when Grandpa emptied his pockets."

"Today, you'd be lucky to get a reaction like that from most kids if you bought them an iPhone," Tom interjected.

"You're probably right," Dan replied, continuing his story. "You know, I'm not sure if it was his nature or his circumstances—probably both—but my dad had a wonderful, simple wisdom that made him seem so real and so earnest."

"Sounds like he was a remarkable man," Tom replied.

"That's why I was struck by some of the things you said," Dan said. "They reminded me of how he used to talk. He would've loved your comment that we need to approach people as the source of the solution rather than the cause of the problem. Sounded just like him."

"That's actually what's struck me most about the ideas I've been thinking about lately," Tom replied. "They have sort of an elemental ring of truth to them."

"That's partly why they're so appealing," said Dan. "I don't know if you've ever read anything by Thoreau, but he preached about the importance of simplicity with the same kind of passion you had earlier today. In one of his books, he said, 'Our life is frittered away by detail. Simplify, simplify. As you simplify your life, the laws of the universe will be simpler.' That idea has had a big influence on my life."

"He must've been whispering in my ear the past few days," Tom said.

"Could be," said Dan. "He also said, 'This world is but a canvas to our imagination'—and he never even heard of Barney."

"Now I *know* he's been talking to me," Tom said with a chuckle.

"If you'd like, I'll lend you my copy of *Walden* up there," said Dan as he got up and pulled the book from the shelf. "It's not very lighthearted reading—Thoreau wasn't exactly a fun-loving guy—but I think you'll like it."

"Thanks, Dan. Maybe it'll give me more insight into the thoughts about human nature that have been buzzing around in my head for the past couple of weeks."

"So let me ask you something," Dan began. "If the secret to getting to the heart of people is really so basic, why is it so tough to get everyone pulling in the same direction? When we get glimpses into those truths about what works with people, why do we have such a hard time staying on that path?"

"I think it's partly because of what I said about processes," said Tom. "On one hand, they're great because they create consistent behavior and predictable results—but they can also get us stuck in some very deep ruts."

"Being an engineer, I tend to think of it as inertia," said Dan. "We invest so much energy in moving in a set direction, and trying to change it is really difficult. That's why I liked your idea about making a *habit* out of improvement, making it part of everyone's everyday job."

"I think another obstacle is that we don't fully appreciate how much we lose when we curb those special qualities of imagination and free will that make human beings so unique," Tom added.

"I don't know about the other folks in the room," said Dan. "But you really rocked me with your comment that imagination without free will has no power, and free will without imagination has no purpose. We really need to spend some time talking about what that means for how we manage people here."

"I'm still trying to flesh that out myself," Tom replied. "But I'm clear about one thing. If we don't get our heads around those ideas, if we don't understand the significance of free will and imagination in the workplace and how they relate to each other, we'll just stay stuck in our ruts and keep spinning our wheels."

"How would you describe those ruts?"

Tom glanced out the window for a few seconds, thinking about how to respond.

"Well, lots of ways," he began slowly. "I think we'll continue trying to put square pegs in round holes, and then we'll get angry and confused when people don't perform the way we want. We'll try to persuade people to do what we want them to do instead of discovering what already motivates them and aligning those motivations with the needs of the organization. When employees look like they're resisting change, we'll interpret it as stubbornness and inflexibility rather than a basic desire to have a measure of control over their lives. We'll complain that employees are aren't coming up with enough fresh ideas on how to improve things, and then we'll blame it on them instead of the policies and systems that get in their way. We'll keep expecting people to do one thing and watch them do something else, and we'll wonder why they won't do it the way we want. And, of course, we'll believe that most people would rather be somewhere else than on the job, and then we'll create the very kind of work environment that makes that belief a self-fulfilling prophecy."

"For someone who's still trying to get his head around this stuff, you sound like you're ready to go on the road with it," said Dan.

"It's pretty easy to see what the downside will be if we can't get a handle on it," Tom replied. "The tough question is figuring out exactly what to do and how to do it."

"During your interview, you talked about needing to balance imagination and free will with the need to keep people aligned and maintain control in the organization. Remember that?" Dan asked.

Tom nodded.

"Well, I think a lot of your ideas for improving communication and for giving more decision-making authority to frontline supervisor can go a long way toward helping us strike that balance."

"I do, too," Tom agreed. "But like you said a moment ago, we have to figure out how to overcome the inertia of the way we're doing things now. Even when you know micromanaging isn't the way to get the best results, it's hard to break that habit."

"Here I go sounding like an engineer again, but part of the challenge for people is sorting out constants from variables and getting consensus on what those are," said Dan. "Truth is, people change, markets change, times change, the world changes—and we have to get in step with those changes."

"Even when the things we've done have been successful," Tom added quickly, "which is usually the toughest time of all to get people to change."

"Absolutely," Dan agreed, pausing momentarily before he continued. "On the other hand, some things stay pretty much the same. Everyone needs air to breathe and water to drink. And like you said, they need security and self-esteem. We have to get a clear common view on those pillars of constancy—core values, sense of purpose, stuff like that. Then we need plans and procedures for adapting to everything else, including the fact that all people mess up sometimes—even the best of them."

"For whatever it's worth, I think the measure of a person's honor isn't in avoiding the stumble, but getting up after the fall," Tom said. "I'd sure like to see if we can find a way to get over the knee-jerk reactions a lot of us have when people make good-faith errors."

"The founder of IBM, Tom Watson, used to say, 'If you want to increase your success rate, double your failure rate,'" Dan said. "I can't say that's part of the routine dialogue we have in our executive committee meetings. But maybe if I share that quote from someone like Watson with them, we can at least start the conversation."

"Going back to what you said a minute ago, though, I think you're right. We have to start with getting everyone on board with—what did you call it—the pillars of constancy?"

"It's sort of like a theory of unified management that underlies all the best practices," Dan replied. "That's why I was so intrigued by what we discussed during your interview today. I take a fair amount of ribbing from the executive committee because I'm an engineer. I think in terms of process, equations, factor analysis, that sort of thing, and I'm the only one on the senior team with that kind of background. I know there are principles—elemental truths, to use your language—that underlie everything that gets applied in engineering. I think your ideas come as close as anything I've heard in a long time to getting a handle on that distinction—between constants and variables in terms of people—in a way that can help us improve employee engagement."

"What's it going to take to convince you that I'm the right person to lead that effort in HR?" Tom asked, somewhat surprised at his leaping out with the question.

Dan started to speak and then seemed to change his thoughts in midstream. He paused and pointed to the bookshelf in the corner.

"I made that as a gift for my dad's sixtieth birthday," said Dan. "Back in high school when I saw my brother's reaction to the carving I made of his name, I knew I'd found my calling. I loved working with wood, and I never got over it. I even thought about making it a profession. But the engineering bug bit me in college, so I've just done it as a hobby all these years."

"It's a beautiful piece of work."

"Thanks," Dan said, "but I wasn't fishing for compliments. I was using it to illustrate a point you made in your interview. Do you remember when you talked about the difference between aptitude, knowledge, and skill?"

"Yes, of course," said Tom, wondering where Dan was going with his question.

"You said when it comes to aptitude, it's important to make sure that you're not trying to put a square peg in a round hole," Dan continued. "Well, if there's ever been a perfect fit between a peg and a hole, it's between me and woodworking. This afternoon, I saw another perfect fit—between you and the VP position in human resources and employee communication."

Tom had prepared himself for the possibility that he wouldn't get the job. But he wasn't ready for how it would hit him if he got it. He was surprised at how touched he was by Dan's comments, and he wasn't sure how to respond.

"Thanks, Dan. I'm flattered," he finally replied. "I'm also pretty moved right now, to be honest with you."

"It's obvious that you have a big personal stake in what you want to do here," Dan said. "You're probably also feeling a lot of responsibility for making it work. But I want you to know, you've got a lot of support behind you."

"I do have to ask if it was a unanimous decision," said Tom. "Some people in there might have thought I'd gone off the deep end with some of the stuff I was saying."

"Not at all," said Dan. "Everyone's pretty excited about what they heard from you, and they can't wait to see you take it on. That's why I asked you to wait in my office. I could tell it wasn't going to take us long to decide you were the guy we needed. They didn't even want to talk anymore about the other candidates."

"It's going to be quite a ride," said Tom. "Do you think they're ready for it?"

"They're terrific people," Dan replied. "They're just as eager as you to make this the kind of company where employees brag a bit more about how great it is to work here."

"It's going to take us a while, and we're going to stumble along the way," Tom said. "But I know one thing we'll have to do to keep us on track."

"What's that?"

"Along with clarity and commitment on those constants you talked about, we'll need systems and processes to keep us aligned and maintain momentum," Tom replied. "We'll also need to hold one another accountable for staying true to our plan. We just have to be patient and persistent. You know what they say, 'Practice makes perfect.'"

"My dad always jumped on people when they used that cliché," Dan replied. "'Practice makes *permanent*,' he would say. It only makes *perfect* if you're practicing the right thing."

"Maybe we can count on your dad's wisdom to give us a little guidance when we want to make sure we're on the right track," said Tom with a warm smile. "Put him alongside Barney and Thoreau, and we've got quite a team of advisors, don't you think?"

"I can only imagine," Dan replied.

"Oh, you can do a lot more than that," said Tom. "But that's a good place to start."

"Well, we'll have to start tomorrow," said Dan. "Right now, I have to do something that is decidedly unimaginative—go over the quarterly financial reports."

"How do the numbers look for the quarter?" asked Tom.

"They're not too bad," Dan replied. "But I'm looking forward to the day when we set the industry standard with the help of our new employee engagement plans," he added with a smile.

"You can count on it," said Tom.

As he got up to leave, Tom caught a glimpse of the carving of Dan's name once again. "By the way," he said, "what ever happened to the piece you did for your brother? Did he keep it?"

"Believe it or not, he has it on his desk, too," Dan replied. "It's kind of a thing that keeps us both in touch with our time together as teenagers. Naturally, I never miss a chance to let him know how much nicer his name looks than mine. Once in a while, I even threaten to take the one I did for him back and rework it to change the name from Don to Dan."

"Another 'D' name, eh?"

"Yeah," Dan replied as the two men walked toward the door. "And we have another brother named Darren. My parents thought it would be fun to keep our initials all the same. Dad's name was David."

Tom stopped dead in his tracks. "What's wrong?" Dan asked.

A flood of thoughts raced through Tom's mind in the split second that it took him to recover.

"Oh, nothing really," he finally said, deciding that his dream was something he wanted to keep to himself. "It's just that I have a friend named David who's been quite an inspiration to me lately."

"Quite a coincidence," said Dan.

"I'm not so sure," Tom said, pausing for a moment as he thought about what he wanted to say next. "Dan, when we create the kind of company that all of us want here—and I'm convinced we will," he added emphatically, "I'd like to ask you to do something for me."

"What's that?"

"I'd like it if you'd make a carving of my name that I can put on my desk," Tom said. "Every time I look at it, it'll remind me of our commitment to getting the very best that people can contribute here."

"Tom, if we pull off what we want to do here, I'll carve a life-size statue of you and put it on the front lawn," said Dan as both men laughed.

"Better yet," Tom replied. "Let's put a statue of Barney out there."

"And we'll inscribe under it 'Imagination without free will has no power. Free will without imagination has no purpose,'" Dan added. "That should get everyone's attention, don't you think?"

As their laughter subsided, Tom reached out to shake Dan's hand.

"I can't tell you how much I appreciate this opportunity, Dan," he said. "It's truly a dream come true—more than you know."

"You've earned it, Tom—and it's not just for you," replied Dan. "Remember, you're not the only one with dreams around here."

"I think there's a song in there somewhere," Tom said trying to lighten the moment.

"If you can have it ready for our annual meeting, we can probably work you into the program for a short performance," Dan replied with a smile in return.

"Oh, that oughta do wonders for shareholder confidence," Tom joked.

"Sounds like you're a square peg in a round hole when it comes to singing," said Dan.

"You can't even imagine," Tom replied.

"Sure, I can," said Dan smiling warmly and pausing for an instant as he put his hand on Tom's shoulder. "Like you said—it's just human nature."

The world is but a canvas to our imagination.
(Henry David Thoreau)

Epilogue

The famed communication theorist Marshall McLuhan once said, "Propaganda ends where dialogue begins." While some companies have made an effort to improve communication, in other organizations today, the sanitizing and glamorizing of information in messages passed down from on high to workers below makes a mockery of McLuhan's appeal.

Why the charade persists is something of a mystery. In the past fifty years, a number of organizational experts have offered considerable wisdom on both the reasons and the methods for optimizing the connections between systems and people. Yet despite the lessons they have shared, employees remain largely disenchanted and disengaged.

Few people like the situation, least of all people like Tom Payton, who take most of the heat for being out of touch with the realities of people in day-to-day operations. Almost everyone knows it is a problem, and they want to make it better. They come to work every day wanting to do a good job and contribute to the success of their organizations—and then they get derailed by misguided management.

While efforts are being made by some organizations to resolve the employee engagement quandary, many companies persist in pursuing a pointless path. They send more messages, create more media, hold more meetings—inadvertently adding more problems and reinforcing a fundamentally flawed paradigm. Instead, they should be rethinking the processes and reinventing the systems for getting employees tuned in and turned on to a high-performance culture that serves employees and organizations alike.

The lessons from *Getting to the Heart of Employee Engagement* come from decades of observing ordinary people in their everyday jobs, and listening to their simple yet insightful wisdom about how to make things work better. Helen Keller captured the significance of their contributions with these eloquent words:

> I long to accomplish great and noble tasks, but it is my chief duty to accomplish humble tasks as though they were great and noble. The world is moved along, not only by the mighty shoves of its heroes, but also by the aggregate of the tiny pushes of each honest worker.

In the spirit of McLuhan's message and in the interest of "each honest worker," we are eager to continue the dialogue about the ideas raised in this book. If you would like to participate in that dialogue, here's how to reach us:

Landes & Associates
3531 Flora Ct.
St. Louis, MO 63104
314-664-6497
leslandes@landesassociates.com
www.landesassociates.com

Appendix A
Core Concepts

The core concepts and operating principles that appear in *Getting to the Heart of Employee Engagement* are summarized here for the reader's convenience.

The Basic Foundation of Elemental Truths

Imagination and free will are uniquely human capabilities that are fundamentally useless without one another. Imagination without free will has no *power*. Free will without imagination has no *purpose*. Both are essential and interrelated forces underlying the full potential of employee engagement in the workplace. Any policy, process, system, or structure that undermines the capacity of people to exercise those extraordinary human gifts in the workplace will inevitably limit people's potential to contribute to the success of the enterprise.

Truths about Human Nature in the Workplace

- People want to do a good job.
- People want to be on a winning team.
- People want to be included and appreciated for their individual contributions.
- People have an innate desire to improve.
- People resist force and uncertainty more than they resist change.
- People assume greater responsibility when they are treated as adults.

Realities about People in the Workplace

- People view the world differently from one another.
- People have "bad hair days" sometimes.
- People make mistakes.
- People have old habits that die hard.
- People often don't have the skills to avoid and resolve conflicts.

Steps for Getting the Best from People in the Workplace

- Be sure the person has the necessary aptitude, knowledge, and skills.
- Encourage continuous learning and development.
- Set clear goals and expectations.
- Provide meaningful rationales and explanations of the benefits.
- Involve employees in determining how to accomplish tasks.
- Align their actions with clearly defined processes.
- Provide the support structure employees need to complete tasks.
- Establish effective guidance and measurement systems.
- Use constructive accountability.
- Be patient and reinforcing.

Factors for Building Employee Trust in Management

- Caring
- Honesty and openness
- Responsiveness
- Competence
- Reliability
- Apology and accountability

Principles of Real-Life, Real-Time Communication

- Interaction
- Availability of information
- Access to information
- Speed
- Relevance
- Inclusion
- Authenticity

Appendix B
The ImaginAction System

M any organizations have some type of program in place for employees to voice their ideas for improvement. Most of those programs, though, fall far short of the substantial potential that exists for getting employees engaged in systematic continuous improvement efforts. Why is that? After all, isn't that what employees want—an opportunity to be heard and to have people take their suggestions seriously? And isn't that what management wants—a way to get everyone contributing to improving the performance of the organization at every level?

As with many "good ideas," the devil is in the details, and after many years of working with numerous organizations, the team at Landes & Associates has identified what works and what doesn't work when it comes to engaging employees in systematic continuous improvement. Those lessons have been incorporated into the design of The ImaginAction System, an improvement process that has proven to be a significant source for increases in performance and profitability.

The Early Days of Employee Suggestions

The earliest documented accounts of efforts to generate improvement ideas from citizens and workers go back to the 1700s in Sweden, Italy, the United Kingdom, and of course Japan.

The first widely recognized employee suggestion program in the United States was developed in the 1890s by John Patterson, the legendary founder of NCR. He called his program the "Hundred-Headed Brain," and his goal went against conventional management wisdom of the day. He wanted a way to get good ideas from all employees without them being stolen or squashed by supervisors, who in those days were even more controlling than today's typical managers. Following the lead set by NCR, countless companies implemented similar programs, a trend which has continued with varying degrees of enthusiasm and success to this day.

The basic premise underlying the traditional suggestion program seems simple and sensible enough. Put a box on the wall or a link on the company website, ask employees to submit their ideas for making an improvement, and then give them rewards if their ideas get implemented. Easy as one, two, three, right? So, why have the vast majority of employee suggestion programs produced such mediocre results?

The Program Trap

Like a lot of other people-related practices in the workplace, the forces that compel employees to go outside their daily routine and offer suggestions for improvement are wrapped up in tangle of complex emotions and expectations. Employees typically give a few standard responses when asked why they don't participate in suggestion programs:

- They just want me to do my job.
- No one really cares or listens.
- My opinions and ideas don't really matter to the company.
- I might get in trouble.
- I'm too busy with my regular work.
- It's too much of a hassle.
- My ideas aren't big enough to make much difference.
- They probably won't accept my ideas anyway.
- They think they know more than I do.
- It takes forever and a day to get something approved.

Those comments point to a fundamental flaw in the way most suggestion programs are designed and implemented. Rather than being woven into the fabric of day-to-day operations, they are seen as one-off activities that are secondary to the "real" work that organizations expect people to do every day. It's a classic example of what we call the program trap: the persistent fixation on jargon, symbols, and rituals over substance and systems.

Few corporate experiments of the past illustrate the hazards of the program trap more compellingly than total quality management (TQM). During the heyday of TQM in the 1990s, when people were being inundated with every manner of quality programs, people often commented, "I don't have time for all of this quality stuff on top of my regular job."

Despite determined efforts to get people tuned in to recognizing that "this quality stuff" *was* part of their regular work, TQM dwindled away. It wasn't because the *ends* lacked merit but because the *means* were tangential to the mainstream of day-to-day business operations. Ironically, many people recognized the disconnect, and they tried valiantly to overcome it—with little success.

One reason they failed is because they were trying to make *system* changes using *program* tools and techniques. Using the human body as a metaphor, they tried to strap TQM on the side of the organizational body as a third leg, pretending that walking down the hall with three legs was as natural as walking with two.

The lesson from that experience is vital and elemental. Unless and until senior management puts continuous improvement in a prominent spot on the corporate agenda, it will never become *systemic*. And until it does, any efforts at engaging employees in making improvements will be, by definition, *dis-continuous*. And anything that is discontinuous eventually becomes irrelevant, a victim of the program trap. It's a logical—and painfully predictable—progression.

Processes and Habits

Another reason it can be challenging to get employees looking at new and better ways to do things on a routine basis is that a process works in essentially the same way as a habit. As we all know, there are good habits and processes, and there are bad habits and processes. One thing, however, is true about *all* habits and processes: unless something is in place to break the repetitive cycles, they will never change; and unless that cycle breaker is an imbedded process itself, the old ways of doing things are likely to return.

The ImaginAction System produces continuous systematic improvement, not just occasional one-off improvement activities. In effect, it becomes a new habit that replaces the old habit of doing things the same way over and over again. Without that kind of systemic design, the likelihood of employees engaging in continuous improvement over time is very slim.

The ImaginAction System

Breaking free from the program trap requires determination and vigilance. Even once the grip of this trap has been loosened, the tendency to slip back into it is ever present. In part, that's because it is so insidious and alluring—that's why it's a trap. The keys to resisting the tendency to backslide are actually quite simple to understand but often challenging to implement. As with any type of people processes, though, slight variances one way or the other can spell the difference between success and failure.

What's in a name? A lot!

When it comes to escaping the flaws of traditional suggestion programs, the first imperative is to change the language. For starters, the word *program* should be avoided entirely and replaced with more integrated and organic terms like *process* and *system*.

Next, get rid of the word *suggestion*. It's too flimsy and tentative to be a formal, integral part of an organization's essential systems and processes. The *ImaginAction System* is designed to be a systemic process rather than a discontinuous program. Furthermore, as its name implies, the purpose of the system is not to generate suggestions, but rather to take action and produce implemented improvements. In the end, the best name to call it inside an organization is something simple and straightforward like the *continuous improvement system*.

Of course, merely changing the description or the name alone will not transform a program into a systemic process any more than naming your child Tiger will turn him into a great golfer. Nevertheless, language does matter, and it is a simple and logical place to start to get people oriented in the right direction.

Basic Building Blocks

The fundamental elements underlying an effective system that generates large numbers of improvements boil down to the following points:

1. **Ease:** Make the process easy and efficient.
2. **Accountability:** Put the responsibility for reviewing and approving the vast majority of potential improvements in the hands of supervisors who are close to the action, and hold them—rather than a manager or suggestion committee—accountable.
3. **Engaged Participation:** Encourage employees to participate, and then respond to their ideas quickly and supportively.
4. **Ownership:** Give employees the responsibility for implementing their own improvement ideas and requesting support from their supervisors and others where needed.
5. **Rewards and Recognition:** Use a reward structure that values all improvements equally regardless of size or value. Offer modest rewards so the main focus is on improvements and informal recognition, not costly incentives.

Perhaps the most significant and surprising aspect of The ImaginAction System is its emphasis on small improvements. The reason is simple. Creating a culture that embraces improvement practices as part of the daily fabric of the organization's lifeblood requires frequent repetition. Large improvement opportunities are rare in most organizations, or they are too complex for most employees to undertake. So they tend to be small in number and are usually handled as special management projects instead of routine employee activities. When the focus is on the "little things that count," each employee's span of influence is expanded, everyone can contribute, and the number of improvements increases dramatically.

That's not to say that big ideas and large improvements are unimportant. To the contrary, The ImaginAction System emphasizes the value of *all* improvements regardless of size. That feature makes the system an ideal complement to lean and Six Sigma initiatives, which tend to focus on larger improvements involving smaller numbers of employees.

If you question the merits of emphasizing, documenting, and rewarding small improvements, ask yourself this question: What kind of impact would it have on your organization's performance if every single employee was aware of and improved all the little things they have control over every day? In the long run, the implementation of hundreds or even thousands of small improvements can have far greater impact on both the culture and the bottom line than a few dozen large projects that involve relatively few employees.

That goal is accomplished using another feature of The ImaginAction System that often raises eyebrows. Whenever an employee implements an improvement, his or her name is entered into a random drawing (one entry per improvement regardless of the size or value of that improvement). Using that approach, all employees have an equal opportunity to win rewards, regardless of the size and value of the improvements they implement. Once again, the main purpose is to create a culture of continuous improvement rather than a competition to win the largest incentives. Importantly, the rewards are relatively modest so the focus is on the intrinsic value and motivation of making improvements more than on the incentives themselves.

The Process

Building on those basic principles, here are the steps and criteria for designing an effective employee improvement system and getting it operational.

Step 1: Preparation for Implementation

1. Provide training and direction for supervisors, who are the principal players in the review and approval process. In general, supervisors must learn how to use process improvement techniques and how to be effective coaches, providing encouragement and support for employees in pursuing improvement opportunities on a daily basis. One particularly important coaching skill for supervisors to learn is how to redirect seemingly off-target or inappropriate ideas without criticizing or discouraging employees' efforts.

a. Conduct learning sessions for all employees that explain procedures for participating in the process and cover the following points:

b. Improvements of all sizes are accepted and are valued equally for the opportunity to win rewards.

c. Employees should focus improvement efforts on areas where they have the greatest knowledge and over which they have some measure of control.

d. Employees should look for opportunities in any aspect of any process that can make work easier, faster, cheaper, better, or safer, and should focus on removing time, materials, or resources from all processes.

e. The organization's key performance indicators (KPIs) should guide everyone's improvement efforts along the entire chain of idea generation, approval, and implementation.

f. Improvements that will streamline or strengthen a process, not just fix an isolated problem, are a priority.

g. Employees should get approval and support for implementing ideas from their immediate supervisors, who are equipped and expected to help with employee improvement efforts.

Step 2: Creation of Reward Structure

1. Set up periodic random drawings (weekly, bi-weekly, or monthly).

2. Establish a modest yet meaningful amount to award to drawing winners. (Non-monetary awards with value between twenty-five and fifty dollars are recommended.)

3. Enter an employee's name into the drawing once for each implemented improvement, with possible options:

    a. Enter a name multiple times for improvements made in designated high-priority areas, such as safety, waste control, etc.

    b. Enter the names of multiple people for the same improvement if more than one person worked on it.

4. Establish the percent of total names entered that will be drawn as winners (between 10 and 20 percent is ideal, depending on the size of the organization).

5. Conduct quarterly reviews, acknowledging the results and conducting further drawings for unusually high levels of participation.

6. Establish the number of implemented improvements for which an individual will qualify for the annual hall of fame (ten to fifteen per year is recommended).

7. Establish separate reward systems for supervisors so they are not competing with employees in the drawings.

Step 3: Process Mechanics

1. When employees have ideas for improvements, they discuss them with their immediate supervisors.

2. Supervisors review these ideas and respond to each employee in one of the following ways:

    a. Give approval and ask the employee if he or she requires assistance in getting the improvement implemented.

    b. Give provisional approval, pending review with other people who may be affected by the proposed improvement.

    c. Advise the employee on adjustments that need to be made before the idea can be implemented.

    d. Explain why the idea cannot be implemented and why it does not qualify for the entry into the drawing.

    e. Forward to senior management or lean/Six Sigma directors ideas that are too big for the supervisors to handle.

3. Employees are given ownership and responsibility for implementing their improvements, requesting support from their supervisors, and getting other employees involved as needed.

4. After an improvement has been implemented, the responsible employee completes a form that describes what was been done and gives the form to his or her supervisor.

5. Supervisors sign these forms and submits them to the process administrator, who takes the following actions:
    a. Logs the improvements into a shared database; and
    b. Enters name(s) into the drawing for that period.
    c. Names that are not drawn for that period are not carried over to the next drawing; new implemented improvements are required for each drawing.

Step 4: After the Drawing

1. Post the names of drawing winners in prominent locations.
2. Supervisors review all improvements logged into the database so they can be examined for possible replication in other areas.

Impact on Supervisors

Among the many benefits of The ImaginAction System is the way it shifts the role of supervisors from scheduler, assignment giver, or referee to coach and mentor. For starters, supervisors are the initial approval point for the vast majority of improvement ideas that employees initiate. That gives them an opportunity to engage with employees in a way that goes beyond the monitoring and directing style of management that characterizes the typical supervisor-worker relationship.

In addition, some ideas brought to supervisors will not be quite on target initially, which gives them the opportunity to provide direction to employees on how to shape them in ways that make them more workable. What's more, these interactions allow supervisors to acknowledge employees for their contributions and thank them for participating in the process. (Compare those dynamics with dropping an idea in a suggestion box for someone to pick up and run through the typical suggestion committee!)

Beyond the opportunity the process affords to improve the working relationships between supervisors and the employees who report to them, the process is also an excellent tool for supervisors to accomplish their own goals. It is appropriate and even encouraged for supervisors to guide employee improvement efforts toward the priorities that the supervisor has set for his or her area of responsibility. That way, supervisors have a built-in incentive for supporting employee participation in the system.

To ensure that employees maintain a continuous focus on the improvement process, supervisors are also encouraged to include discussions about improvements during regularly scheduled team meetings. That's one way to ensure that the process is seen as an integral part of day-to-day work as opposed to an occasional sidebar activity.

Since the work of the supervisor is so critical to the system's success, specific requirements for supporting the improvement process should be included in the job descriptions of all supervisors. Likewise, specific objectives and expectations should be set for supervisor performance in engaging employees who report to them in the improvement process.

Role of Senior Management

Although members of the senior management team have limited involvement in the day-to-day activities of the system, they still play an important role in its ongoing effectiveness. That role begins with placing review and discussion of the system on the agenda of standing senior management meetings. After performance targets have been established, those numbers should be reviewed by senior management with the same scrutiny and regularity given to other key metrics and indicators.

Just as supervisors are encouraged to focus employee improvement attention on department priorities, senior managers should identify goals and priorities that employees can help the organization achieve. That attention provides focus for improvements and justification for investment in the system.

On a periodic basis, senior managers should also communicate directly with employees about the improvement process, preferably through existing regular meetings and communication venues. During those sessions, management should emphasize the importance of employee improvements in achieving company goals. They should also reinforce the value of focusing on small improvements that employees can control in their areas of responsibility. Celebrating and acknowledging contributions being made by employees participating in the process is important as well.

Since The ImaginAction System is designed to generate ideas for improvements of all sizes, senior management can help prioritize and implement larger improvements that are beyond the scope of what supervisors may authorize and manage on their own.

Hardwiring the System

Aside from making the system a core element in all department discussion meeting and management agendas, other things can be done to hardwire the process into daily operations:

1. Include the role and responsibility for the improvement process in each person's job description.
2. Make participation in the improvement process part of all performance reviews.
3. Link participation in the improvement process to company, department, and individual bonuses.
4. Guide improvement efforts to focus on key performance indicators (KPIs) that are tied to company goals and priorities.
5. Make continuous improvement part of all discussions and meeting agendas related to organizational performance.

A note of caution here: While participation in the improvement process should be strongly encouraged and supported, it should not be mandatory. And while management should set aggressive goals for participation levels, be wary of setting quotas for the number of improvements or the financial impact that they are expected to have. You have to be extremely vigilant that the improvement process is used as a carrot, not a club; otherwise, employees will eventually resent the process and stop participating altogether.

The Payoff

Results from The ImaginAction System vary depending on numerous factors. Increases of 200 to 600 percent in the number of implemented improvements over previous programs are not uncommon. The average number of improvements per employee varies greatly from a low of two implemented improvements per year per employee (still higher than in most suggestion programs) to an average high of fifty implemented improvements per employee per year.

Another important participation metric is the percent of employees who implement at least one improvement annually. With the typical suggestion program, that rate is about 5-15 percent. With The ImaginAction System, the number of participating employees each year runs from a low of 50 percent to a high of 85 percent.

In general, organizations that excel with the system are the ones that embrace all the essential characteristics for integrating the process systemically into daily operations. They also tend to be organizations that are determined to achieve significant culture change and see the improvement process as a core mechanism for engaging all employees in the change effort.

One thing is common among all organizations that succeed with The ImaginAction System regardless of the level of improvement they achieve. They are not looking merely to tweak and rev up their existing programs; rather, they are committed to developing a system for improvement that produces breakthrough results across the organization.

Appendix C
Mission Control

Most people are familiar with the saying "What gets measured is what gets done." That is only partly true. How people *communicate* about those measurements also determines not only what gets done, but how efficiently and effectively people do it. As a practical matter, it is challenging for most organizations to figure out how to share relevant information in a way that is timely, readily accessible to employees, and actionable.

The solutions vary depending on the nature of the information and the intended stakeholder group. But for the essential operating information that is relevant to all employees, Landes & Associates offers a tool that has proven to be highly effective for numerous organizations, including winners of the Baldrige National Quality Award.

We call it Mission Control.

Just like its NASA namesake, Mission Control has some special features that make it particularly effective for monitoring and managing performance in the workplace. First, it helps to prioritize, organize, and visualize performance data, and it provides a mechanism for displaying big-picture connections among key data indicators. More important— and this is where Mission Control differs from most dashboards and scorecards—it provides a proactive alert system for not only sharing data on key indicators, but also for taking corrective action when it is required.

So how do you ensure that meaningful data are woven into the fabric of the organization's day-to-day operations? First, identify the macro indicators that apply to the organization as a whole, such as:

- Business growth goals
- Employee engagement
- Quality
- Productivity
- Customer satisfaction
- Financials

Characteristics of an Effective System

In establishing effective metrics, organizations have to establish, monitor, and report on both leading and lagging indicators. Leading indicators measure inputs or performance; lagging indicators measure outcomes or results.

Sometimes, it can be unclear which indicators are leading and which ones are lagging. All indicators exist on a continuum, and all of them are leading and lagging indicators depending on what they come before or after. The further an indicator is to the leading edge of the continuum, the more direct control people can exert on it; the further to the lagging edge of the continuum, the less control people have.

The key to exerting legitimate and effective control over outcomes is using leading indicators with high predictive value, and then designing the system so that it adjusts itself according to the data and information that the indicators generate.

Managing an effective dual-purpose measurement and communication system requires the cooperative involvement of multiple functions within the organization—communication, human resources, organizational development, finance, quality, information technology, sales, marketing, customer service, and others.

The roles played by the people in this measurement and communication orchestra vary depending on numerous factors. Someone, though, has to take the lead and serve as the conductor who keeps the group operating in unison. Regardless of who plays what role on that cross functional team, several important elements have to be built into the design of the system.

- **Frequent and Timely**

  The more frequently the data are gathered and examined, the greater the opportunity to make adjustments and take corrective actions for continuous improvement. Frequency is especially important for the leading indicators over which people have direct control so that corrective action can be taken to steer the process back on course before the impact becomes too severe and costly.

- **Simple**

  Simplicity is important on two levels. First, the data must be accessible and easy to gather. If it takes too much time and effort to capture data, people will resist the effort to compile it. Second, key data must be presented in a way that people can understand without being overwhelmed. Make the data clear, and don't give people so much that they can't effectively process it or act on it.

- **Visual and Visible**

  Remember the old saying, "out of sight, out of mind." When data are displayed openly, using highly visual tools like charts, shapes, and colors, they are much more likely to draw attention. Effective displays also make it easier to activate a response than if information is distributed selectively to managers in periodic reports, which are then tucked away in file folders and binders. High visibility helps to create a collective and continuous consciousness about organizational priorities and how the organization is performing. It also prompts corrective action more effectively when the numbers fall below established benchmarks.

- **Relevant and Connective**

  It can be a big challenge to connect individual goals, interests, and priorities with those of the organization. If people don't appreciate the relevance and value of the data, or if they can't see how their work can have a measurable impact on those data points, it is difficult to get them excited about doing anything with it. That means they need their own micro measures to guide individual or small-group performance, and those micro measures must link clearly to the common macro measures of the overall system.

It is important to remember that different types of data will be more or less relevant to various groups and individuals, depending on their roles in the organization. The key is to make sure that people see and understand the data that are most important to each of them. It is also vital to make sure that at least some of the major, macro data—both leading and lagging indicators—are relevant to everyone so there is a shared sense of purpose and focus throughout the organization.

Examples of macro measures might be safety, employee learning and development, results of continuous improvement efforts, quality of products and services, defect and rework rates, results of employee opinion surveys, customer satisfaction, sales and margins, progress reports on employee profit sharing, and the like.

- **Quantitative**

  Numbers may not tell the whole story about organizational performance, but they provide an effective common language for evaluation and corrective action. Without that common language, people throughout the organization will have different perceptions of organizational and individual performance. What's more, even with "soft" factors such as attitude, satisfaction, and trust, it is possible to conduct clear quantitative assessment using Lickert scales to rate opinions on a scale of 1 to 5.

- **Benchmarked/Targeted**

  Clearly defined targets are important. They help people know where to aim their efforts and determine whether or not they are hitting the mark. Without those targets, the quality of performance and results comes down to a matter of subjective, individual interpretation, and it becomes difficult to know precisely when to take corrective action.

- **Action-Based**

    In order to get maximum impact, reporting and reviewing data must lead to corrective action when indicators miss the mark. Action plans should be developed in advance to reduce uncertainty or hesitation in reacting when performance and results go awry. Another reason for developing response plans in advance is that the worst time to decide how to respond to a crisis is typically when you are in the middle of it. Anxiety runs high, judgment is impaired, and the resulting decisions and actions can often be suboptimal.

In the end, the value of Mission Control comes down to two simple yet vital factors. First, Mission Control enables everyone to know how the organization's mission is going at all times. Second, it activates a predetermined course of action if performance indicators fall below established benchmarks.

That type of system helps to ensure excellence for any operation whether the goal is a successful space flight or a successful company, and it underscores the fact that organizations typically get what they deserve by the way they design these systems. As the author and social theorist Henry David Thoreau said, "In the end, men always hit what they aim for."

Open Book Management

In countless studies conducted across the world, one core theme continuously emerges as a road block to employee engagement. It's a theme that goes to the core of "mission control." The lack of clarity and access by every employee to the goals and "numbers" of the business is one of the biggest missteps companies continue to make today. The most highly publicized effort to overcome that problem began in 1983 when Springfield Remanufacturing Corporation pioneered what they have called "open book management" (OBM).

Since that time, their living laboratory for communicating with employees about the company's financial information has been studied and scrutinized worldwide. Companies that have been exposed to OBM have discovered two important things. First, opening up the books is neither risky nor complicated. Second, when you do it right, the impact on company performance is akin to what has been described as "lightning in a bottle." The thousands of companies that have embraced that methodology (coined "The Great Game of Business" by SRC CEO Jack Stack) have out-performed their peers significantly on nearly every key financial ratio.

What's more, they tend to have employees who are freer thinkers, faster movers and regularly score higher in term of employee satisfaction and happiness. Taken together, all of the factors related to the OBM methodology – communication patterns, transparency, teaching business literacy, regular meetings by all employees around the financials of the business, and connecting with the heart of people through fun and a "stake in the outcome" – form a compelling force for fostering imagination and free will.

About the Author

L es Landes is president of Landes & Associates based in St. Louis, Missouri. The firm's overriding focus is on helping organizations create the kind of culture where employees love to work and customers love doing business. They provide an array of services that help organizations align employee engagement with marketing communication to improve performance. Landes formerly was the head of corporate communications for a major international food company, and he currently writes a popular e-column called Inside-Out.

Printed in the United States
by Baker & Taylor Publisher Services